101 Practical Tax Tips

2022/23

By
Sarah Bradford

Publisher details

This guide is published by Tax Insider Ltd, 3 Sanderson Close, Great Sankey, Warrington WA5 3LN.

'101 Practical Tax Tips' (formerly 101 Tax Secrets Revealed) first published in July 2010, second edition September 2010, third edition May 2011, fourth edition April 2012, fifth edition May 2012, sixth edition August 2012, seventh edition April 2013, eighth edition April 2014, ninth edition November 2015, tenth edition October 2020, 11th edition August 2021, 12th edition May 2022.

Copyright

All rights reserved

Trademarks

Disclaimer

This guide is produced for general guidance only, and professional advice should be sought before any decision is made. Individual circumstances can vary and therefore no responsibility can be accepted by Tax Insider, the co-author Sarah Bradford, or the publisher Tax Insider Ltd for any action taken or any decision made to refrain from action by any readers of this guide.

Tax rules and legislation are constantly changing and therefore the information printed in this guide is correct at the time of writing — May 2022.

Neither the authors nor Tax Insider Ltd offer financial, legal or investment advice. If you require such advice then we urge you to seek the opinion of an appropriate professional in the relevant field. We care about your success and therefore encourage you to take appropriate advice before you put any of your financial or other resources at risk. Don't forget, investment values can decrease as well as increase.

The content of this guide is for information only and all examples and numbers are for illustration. Professional advice should always be sought before undertaking any tax planning of any sort as individual circumstances vary and other considerations may have to be taken into account before acting.

To the fullest extent permitted by law Sarah Bradford and Tax Insider Ltd do not accept liability for any direct, indirect, special, consequential or other losses or damages of whatsoever kind arising from using this guide.

The guide itself is provided 'as is' without express or implied warranty.

Contents

About This Guide

All taxpayers like to save tax and there are many simple steps that can be taken to achieve this aim.

This guide contains 101 ultimate tax tips. By reading through these practical tips you will come across at least a few that will apply to your circumstances and save you some tax. Or at the very least they have given you food for thought and you will take some professional advice before taking any action or refraining from any action as a result of reading these tips.

The tips are for guidance only and professional advice should always be sought before undertaking tax planning of any sort. The savings that can be made will depend on the precise circumstances and the examples are a guide only.

There are always more tips as tax is a very complex subject. However, this book covers the more practical ideas so that everyone can take something from it.

Chapter 1:
Making The Most Of Allowances And Lower Rates Of Tax

1. Keeping The Full Personal Allowance

2. Make Use Of The Marriage Allowance

3. Utilising Your Annual CGT Exemption

4. Transfer Income-Earning Investments To Use Non-Taxpayers' Personal Allowances

5. Utilising Spouse's Or Civil Partner's Annual CGT Exemption

6. Equalising Marginal Rates Of Tax

1. Keeping The Full Personal Allowance

The personal allowance allows a person to receive the first £12,570 of their income tax-free for 2022/23. This is worthwhile. However, once income exceeds a certain level, the personal allowance may be lost.

For 2022/23 the basic personal allowance is reduced where a person has 'adjusted net income' in excess of £100,000 by £1 for every £2 by which this limit is exceeded until the allowance is fully abated.

This means that anyone with adjusted net income of more than £125,140 in 2022/23 loses all their personal allowance.

However, it is possible to preserve entitlement to the personal allowance by reducing income to below £100,000. There are various ways in which this can be achieved, for example by transferring income-producing assets to a spouse or civil partner (see Tip 4).

Likewise, adjusted net income can be reduced by making pension contributions, which is in itself beneficial due to the higher rate relief that is available on pension contributions up to the available annual allowance. Charitable donations made under gift aid would also work (although the donor would lose the benefit of money made as the donation).

Alternatively, a sole trader or proprietor of an unincorporated business could employ a spouse or civil partner or other family member and pay them a salary to reduce his or her self-employment income, shifting income to the family member.

Note: the personal allowance will remain at £12,570 for future tax years up to and including 2025/26.

Keeping The Full Personal Allowance

John has adjusted net income of £128,000 for 2022/23, of which £30,000 is in the form of interest from investments. His wife has income of £10,000 for the year.

As John has income for 2022/23 in excess of £125,140, he will lose all his personal allowance for that year. By transferring the investments to his wife, his income is reduced to £98,000 and he retains the personal allowance of £12,570. For a higher rate taxpayer paying tax at 40%, the personal allowance is worth £5,028 for 2022/23 (£12,570 x 40%). By transferring income to his wife, John retains his personal allowance.

As he is a higher rate taxpayer, he is entitled to a personal savings allowance of £500. Had he not transferred the investments to his wife, he would have paid tax on the investment income of £11,800 ((£30,000 – £500) x 40%). By transferring the investments, and thus the tax liability on the interest to his wife, he saves tax of £11,800 plus a further £5,000 by retaining the personal allowance. His tax bill is therefore reduced by £16,800 (£11,800 + £5,000).

As far as the £30,000 savings income transferred to his wife is concerned, the first £1,000 is covered by her personal savings allowance of £1,000, the next £2,570 is covered by the remainder of her personal allowance (£12,570 – £10,000) and the next £5,000 is taxed at the savings rate of 0%. The remaining £21,430 (£30,000 – (£1,000 + £2,570 + £5,000)) is taxed at 20% – a tax bill of £4,286.

As a couple, they are £12,514 better off. Although his wife pays an additional £4,286 in tax, John saves tax of £16,800 – a combined saving of £12,514.

2.   Make Use Of The Marriage Allowance

The marriage allowance allows an individual to transfer 10% of his or her personal allowance (rounded up to the nearest £10) to his or her spouse or civil partner, as long as neither pays tax at a rate that is higher than the basic rate of tax.

This measure allows a couple, where one partner does not fully utilise their personal allowance, to give the benefit of some of that allowance to their partner, saving tax of up to 20% of the amount transferred. This is useful where it is not possible to transfer income-producing assets from one spouse or civil partner to the other in order to mop up the personal allowance (see Tip 4).

For 2022/23, the basic personal allowance is £12,570. This means that where neither party pays tax at a rate above the basic rate, the marriage allowance allows £1,260 of the personal allowance to be transferred, making it possible to save tax of up to £252 (£1,260 x 20%).

The transferor's personal allowance is reduced by the amount of the marriage allowance – from £12,570 to £11,310 for 2022/23 – and the transferee's personal allowance is increased by the amount of the marriage allowance, from £12,570 to £13,830 for 2022/23. Each party's tax code is amended – with the M suffix denoting the individual is in receipt of the marriage allowance and the N suffix denoting that the individual has transferred the marriage allowance to their spouse or civil partner.

The allowance cannot be tailored – the transfer is 10% of the allowance rounded up to the nearest £10 or nothing. Where the transferor's income is less than the personal allowance but is more than an amount equal to the personal allowance less the marriage allowance (i.e. between £11,310 and £12,569 for 2022/23), claiming the marriage allowance will still be worthwhile and will save tax, but the saving will be less than £252. The transferee will save £252, but the transferor will pay tax to the extent that his or her income exceeds the amount equal to the personal allowance less the marriage allowance (£11,310 for 2022/23, being the personal allowance of £12,570 less the marriage allowance transferred of £1,260).

Note: the personal allowance will remain at £12,570 and the marriage allowance will remain at £1,260 for tax years up to and including 2025/26.

Make Use Of The Marriage Allowance

Josh and Hannah are married. Hannah does not work as she stays at home to look after their two-year-old son. Josh earns £20,000 a year. They claim the marriage allowance to transfer £1,260 of Hannah's personal allowance for 2022/23 to Josh. As a result, Hannah's personal allowance is reduced to £11,310 (£12,570 – £1,260) and Josh's personal allowance is increased to £13,830 (£12,570 + £1,260). By making the transfer, Josh pays £252 (£1,260 x 20%) less tax.

Harry has income from freelance work of £12,000 in 2022/23. His wife Lily has income of £18,000 from her job as a teaching assistant.

As Harry is unable to utilise £570 of his personal allowance for 2022/23, the couple claim the marriage allowance. Lily's personal allowance is increased to £13,830 and her tax bill is reduced by £252 (£1,260 x 20%). Harry's personal allowance is reduced to £11,310 and, as a result, he must now pay tax on £690 of his income (£12,000 – £11,310), a tax bill of £138 (£690 x 20%). By claiming the marriage allowance, the couple are £114 better off (£252 saved by Lily less the £138 additional tax payable by Harry).

3.   Utilising Your Annual CGT Exemption

If you have significant capital gains within your portfolio then it is important to utilise the annual capital gains tax exempt amount.

For the 2022/23 tax year, this is worth £12,300 per person. Any net gains (after deducting allowable losses) within this figure are exempt from capital gains tax.

As each individual has their own allowance, spouses and civil partners can make gains of £24,600 in 2022/23 before any capital gains tax is payable, using the no gain/no loss rules to transfer assets between them before the sale to ensure that one spouse or civil partner's annual exempt amount is not wasted (see Tip 5).

It is important to remember that the allowance is lost if it is not used in the tax year – it can't be carried forward. Where, for example, an individual has shares to sell, they could use their tax-free allowance each year to sell off just enough shares (or other qualifying assets) to realise a gain equivalent to the annual exemption. Once gains equal to the annual exemption have been realised, any further disposals should ideally be deferred until the following tax year to avoid triggering a capital gains tax liability.

Note: the capital gains tax annual exempt amount will remain at £12,300 for future tax years up to and including 2025/26.

Utilising Your Annual CGT Exemption

Smart John

John has a significant share portfolio and is a higher rate taxpayer.

For 2022/23, he will be liable to capital gains tax at 20% on any chargeable gains (or 28% if from a residential property) in excess of his capital gains tax annual exempt amount of £12,300.

He has held his shares for a number of years and has always made use of his annual exemption for capital gains tax purposes, selling sufficient shares to realise a gain approximately equal to the capital gains tax exempt amount (£12,300 for 2022/23). He makes no further disposals in the tax year once his annual exemption has been utilised.

By utilising his annual exemption for 2022/23, he is able to realise tax-free gains of £12,300. Had he already used his annual exempt amount, he would have had to pay capital gains tax of £2,460 (£12,300 x 20%) on the gain on the shares.

By using his annual exemption each year and only making disposals within the annual exemption rather than disposing of further shares once his annual exemption has been used, he can dispose of his shares without having to pay any capital gains tax.

Not So Smart Jack

Jack does not spread the sale of his shares over several years but instead sells shares and realises gains of £35,000 in 2022/23. He has other income of £60,000. As he is a higher rate taxpayer, he pays capital gains tax at 20%.

The annual exemption of £12,300 is set against the gain of £35,000, leaving net chargeable gains of £22,700. He pays tax on these gains of £4,540 (£22,700 x 20%), leaving him with £30,460 after tax to reinvest.

Compare this with John, who is able to reinvest all his sale proceeds by realising his gains completely tax-free by selling his shares over a number of years and making best use of the annual exempt amount.

4.   Transfer Income-Earning Investments To Use Non-Taxpayers' Personal Allowances

If one spouse or civil partner is working and the other has no taxable income, it is worthwhile considering transferring income-producing investments to the non-working spouse/civil partner in order to utilise their personal allowance if the income would be taxable on the working spouse/civil partner.

This may be an option, for example, if one partner has, say, shares or a property which is rented out. Under the capital gains tax rules for spouses and civil partners, it is possible to transfer assets between spouses on a no gain/no loss basis. This means that assets can be transferred between spouses without triggering a capital gains tax liability.

Where assets are owned jointly, spouses and civil partners are deemed to share the income equally, regardless of the actual ownership of the underlying asset (unless the couple elect on Form 17 for income to be allocated in accordance with the actual beneficial ownership where assets are jointly owned as tenants in common in unequal shares). This rule makes it possible to shift 50% of the income to a spouse or civil partner, while retaining a greater share of the ownership of the underlying asset.

Making use of a spouse or civil partner's unused personal allowance will save tax and will increase the overall post-tax return from the underlying investments. If it is not possible to utilise all of one spouse or civil partner's personal allowance, consider whether the marriage allowance can be claimed (see Tip 3).

Note: the personal allowance will remain at £12,570 for future tax years up to and including 2025/26.

Transfer Income-Earning Investments To Use Non-Taxpayers' Personal Allowances

Mr Smith has two investment properties, yielding rental income of £25,000. Mr Smith is a higher rate taxpayer and pays tax at 40%. Mrs Smith does not work and has no taxable income.

At present, the rental income suffers tax at 40%, giving a tax bill of £10,000 (£25,000 x 40%) and leaving a net amount received after tax of £15,000 (£25,000 – £10,000). By transferring a 5% stake in each property to Mrs Smith, each will be taxed on an income of £12,500.

As they are married, the income is deemed to accrue to them equally for tax purposes, so each is taxed on rental profits of £12,500. Mrs Smith's share of the rental profits are covered by her personal allowance, set at £12,570 for 2022/23. Mr Smith's share will be taxed at 40%, generating a tax bill of £5,000 (£12,500 x 40%) Adopting this strategy reduces the combined tax bill from £10,000 to £5,000, and increases the rental income retained to £20,000.

Mr Smith retains a 95% interest in each property. Mr Smith only needs to give up a small stake in the properties for the couple to be able to reduce the tax paid on the rental income by half. This means that an instant tax saving of £5,000 can be made.

5.   Utilising A Spouse's Or Civil Partner's Annual CGT Exemption

Each spouse or civil partner has their own capital gains tax annual exempt amount. As assets can be transferred between spouses and civil partners at a value that gives neither a gain nor a loss, it is relatively straightforward to ensure best use is made of available annual exempt amounts.

By transferring assets into joint names with your spouse or civil partner prior to sale, or wholly to your spouse or civil partner, you can utilise your spouse's or civil partner's annual capital gains tax exempt amount as well as your own, to the extent that their exempt amount remains available.

For 2022/23, the annual exemption is £12,300, which means that a couple can realise gains of up to £24,600 before paying any capital gains tax.

Transfers between spouses and civil partners are treated as a no gain/no loss transaction and hence the spouse/civil partner to whom the asset is transferred effectively steps into the shoes of the other holder, taking over their base cost and length of ownership.

This can be especially useful when selling investment properties, although Stamp Duty Land Tax (or, in Scotland, Land and Buildings Transaction Tax or Land Transaction Tax in Wales) considerations need to be taken into account if there is any valuable consideration for the sale (which will include taking on a share of a mortgage).

It is necessary to look at the total picture and ensure that any capital gains tax savings are not outweighed by Stamp Duty Land Tax (or equivalent) and any legal costs incurred in transferring ownership of the asset.

Note: the capital gains tax annual exempt amount will remain at £12,300 for future tax years up to and including 2025/26.

Utilising A Spouse's Or Civil Partner's Annual CGT Exemption

Mr Smith (a higher rate taxpayer) wants to sell shares in 2022/23, which will realise a taxable gain of £24,000.

If he goes ahead and sells the shares, after deducting his annual allowance of £12,300, he will pay capital gains tax on £11,700 x 20% = £2,340.

However, if Mr Smith transfers half of the shares to his wife prior to the sale then Mr and Mrs Smith would each have a taxable gain of £12,000, which would be covered by their annual exemption of £12,300.

As each spouse uses £12,000 of their annual exemption for 2022/23 (set at £12,300), the shares can be sold without triggering a capital gains tax liability, leaving them £2,340 better off than if Mr Smith had retained ownership and sold all the shares himself.

6.   Equalising Marginal Rates Of Tax

For 2022/23, there are three rates of income tax for UK taxpayers excluding Scottish taxpayers – the basic rate of 20%, the higher rate of 40% and the additional rate of 45%. For Scottish taxpayers, there are five rates of income tax – the Scottish starter rate of 19%, the Scottish basic rate of 20%, the Scottish intermediate rate of 21%, the Scottish higher rate of 41% and the Scottish top rate of 46%. The Scottish rates apply to the non-savings non-dividend income of Scottish taxpayers. Although income tax in Wales is devolved, for 2022/23 the Welsh rates of income tax (which apply to the non-savings, non-dividend income of Welsh taxpayers) are the same as for the rest of the UK, excluding Scotland.

By transferring income to a lower-earning spouse or civil partner, it is possible to save tax at the higher rates, thereby reducing the combined tax bill.

It should be noted that to transfer income to a spouse or civil partner, the underlying asset, such as shares, must be transferred, rather than the income (for example, the dividend) itself. It must also be remembered that where assets are held jointly by spouses and civil partners, the income is treated as arising equally, even if the asset is owned in unequal shares, unless the couple elects (on Form 17) for the income to be taxed in accordance with the actual underlying ownership.

Where the taxpayer is a sole trader or proprietor of an unincorporated business, employing the spouse or civil partner in the business and paying them a salary will transfer income from one spouse to the other (although, there may be National Insurance to take into account).

It should also be noted that in practice, it will not always be possible to transfer income from one spouse to another, for example, where the spouses are employed and their income is from their employment.

However, where both partners are employed and one pays tax at the additional rate and the other at a lower rate, to minimise their combined tax bill, any investments should be in the name of the lower-earning partner. However, the transferring spouse will lose entitlement to the investment, and consequently the non-tax implications of such a strategy should be borne in mind; the tax tail should not wag the dog.

Equalising Marginal Rates Of Tax

Stuart is an additional rate taxpayer living in London with income of £200,000. His wife Louise has income of £50,000 (after deducting personal allowances).

By transferring assets generating income of £50,000 to his wife, the rate of tax charged on the income from those assets is reduced from 45% (payable by Stuart) to 40% (payable by Louise), saving tax of £2,500 (5% of £50,000).

If Louise had been a basic rate taxpayer, it would be possible to generate greater savings, by transferring sufficient income to use the whole of her basic rate band.

The basic rate band for UK taxpayers excluding Scottish taxpayers is set at £37,700 for 2022/23. The personal allowance is set at £12,570 for 2022/23, making it possible to have income of £50,270 before paying higher rate tax.

It should be noted that the personal allowance is reduced by £1 for every £2 by which income exceeds £100,000. When transferring income to a spouse, care should be taken that the transfer does not take their income above £100,000.

Chapter 2:
Savings and Investments

7.   Use Your Personal Savings Allowance

The personal savings allowance enables basic and higher rate taxpayers to enjoy a certain amount of savings income tax-free. Additional rate taxpayers do not benefit from a personal savings allowance.

For 2022/23, the personal savings allowance is set at £1,000 for basic rate taxpayers and at £500 for higher rate taxpayers; consequently, it is worth £200.

Bank and building society interest is paid gross with no tax deducted by the bank.

To maximise the use of the allowances, savings should be held so as not to waste the allowances; for example, if one spouse is a basic rate taxpayer and the other is an additional rate taxpayer, consideration should be given to holding the savings in the name of the basic rate taxpayer to make use of the allowance.

Use Your Personal Savings Allowance

John and Michelle have combined savings of £150,000, which earn interest of 1% -- equivalent to £1,500 a year. John is a basic rate taxpayer and Michelle is a higher rate taxpayer.

To make use of their personal savings allowances, they arrange their savings so that £50,000 is in Michelle's name and £100,000 is in John's name.

In 2022/23, Michelle, as a higher rate taxpayer, is entitled to a personal savings allowance of £500, and John is a basic rate taxpayer, entitled to a personal savings allowance of £1,000.

Michelle earns interest of £500 on her savings of £50,000 (£50,000 x 1%), which is covered by her personal savings allowance and John earns interest of £1,000 on his savings of £100,000 (£100,000 x 1%), which is covered by his personal savings allowance.

Had the couple held their savings in joint names, each would have been assessed on 50% of the interest arising in the year – £750 each. While this is within John's personal savings allowance and would be received tax-free by him, Michelle's share would exceed her personal savings allowance of £500 and the excess of £250 would be taxed at 40% – generating a tax bill of £100 (£250 x 40%).

By splitting their savings to utilise their differing savings allowances, they can enjoy the interest tax-free. Taking this route means that they are £100 better off than if they had held their savings in joint names.

8.   Use Your ISA Allowance

Although the personal savings allowance will enable most taxpayers to enjoy their savings income tax-free, the ISA allowance provides a second bite at the cherry. It also provides additional rate taxpayers who do not benefit from a savings allowance the option of receiving tax-free savings income. Basic and higher rate taxpayers who have already used up their personal savings allowance can take advantage of an ISA to increase their tax-free savings. Where a stocks and shares ISA is held, the allowance provides the opportunity to enjoy dividends on investments held within the ISA, and any gains on sale, tax-free.

Interest and dividends on cash and investments held within an ISA are tax-free and any gains are free of capital gains tax.

The ISA allowance is available in addition to the personal savings and dividend allowances, and also the 0% starter rate on savings income (see Tip 12). However, investments in a lifetime ISA (see Tip 10) count towards the ISA allowance for the year.

For 2022/23, the ISA limit is set at £20,000. This can be held entirely in cash, entirely in stocks and shares, or as a mix of the two (split however you like as long as total investment in the year does not exceed £20,000). By using your ISA allowance each year, you are able to build up a savings pot on which interest and dividends are tax-free as long as the cash or investments remain in the ISA.

Use Your ISA Allowance

Harry invests £20,000 in a cash ISA on 6 April 2022. This is the maximum he can invest in an ISA in the 2022/23 tax year.

He makes a policy of investing in an ISA up to the ISA limit each year. Interest and dividends on cash and stocks and shares held within the ISA can be enjoyed tax-free. This is in addition to the personal savings allowance and the dividend allowance.

9.   Using ISAs To Save For Retirement

ISAs provide the opportunity to receive tax-free income and gains (see also Tip 8).

By investing in an ISA each year, it is possible to build up a significant pot. For example, using an ISA to invest £10,000 each year for ten years will provide a pot of £100,000 plus accumulated interest and dividends, which also generate tax- free returns.

Over a number of years, investing in an ISA can be a viable alternative to a pension fund, as the proceeds can be taken at any time; there is no requirement to wait for retirement age. Further, there is no limit on the amount that can be withdrawn.

However, unlike contributions to a registered pension scheme, there is no tax relief on ISA subscriptions. However, on the plus side, there is no tax to pay when the funds are withdrawn from the ISA, whereas withdrawals from a pension in excess of the tax-free lump sum are taxed at the individual's marginal rate of tax. Also, there is no need to wait until age 55 to make a withdrawal (individuals can withdraw funds from a money purchase pension plan once they reach the age of 55, without triggering a tax charge on unauthorised withdrawals).

ISAs are also useful for the retention of income within the fund, as this is received tax-free. This means that the fund can grow at a faster rate than if the funds were held outside an ISA where potentially up to 45% of the investment return would be taxed.

A lifetime ISA can also be used to save for retirement (or for the deposit for a first house) (see Tip 10). Amounts saved in a lifetime ISA count towards the overall ISA limit for the tax year.

Using ISAs To Save For Retirement

Craig has invested in a stocks and shares ISA over a number of years

On reaching the age of 50, Craig decides to give up work and cash in 50% of the balance in his ISA. In doing so, he realises a capital gain of £50,000.

The gain is free of capital gains tax. If he had made the investments outside the ISA, he would have been liable for capital gains tax on the gain. Assuming that Craig is a higher rate taxpayer who has used his capital gains tax annual exemption elsewhere, investing within an ISA has saved him capital gains tax of £10,000 (£50,000 x 20%).

ISAs also provide flexibility as to withdrawals, which can be made at any age. There is no need to wait until age 55 as with a registered pension scheme.

10. Make Use Of A Lifetime ISA

A lifetime ISA is a specific type of ISA which can be used either to save for a deposit for a first home or to save for retirement. A lifetime ISA can only be opened by individuals between the ages of 18 and 40, but once a lifetime ISA has been opened, the individuals can continue to invest in it until the age of 50.

An individual can invest up to £4,000 a year in a lifetime ISA; however, any amounts invested in a lifetime ISA count towards the overall ISA limit for the tax year (see Tip 8), set at £20,000 for 2022/23. Thus, an individual could invest £4,000 in a lifetime ISA and up to £16,000 in standard ISA.

Amounts invested in a lifetime ISA attract a government bonus of 25% – a maximum of £1,000 a year where the maximum annual investment of £4,000 is made. Cash, stock and shares or a combination of both can be held in a lifetime ISA.

It is only possible to continue to save in a lifetime ISA (and to receive the government bonus) until the age of 50 (and the account must be opened by the age of 40). On reaching the age of 50, the account can remain open and savings and investments held in the account will continue to earn returns.

The purpose of a lifetime ISA is to help individuals to save for their first home or to save for retirement. Consequently, money can only be withdrawn from an ISA without penalty on buying a first home or once the individual has reached the age of 60. A person who is terminally ill and who has less than 12 months to live can also withdraw funds from a lifetime ISA without penalty. In all other cases, a 25% withdrawal charge normally applies – this will recoup the government bonus and also apply a charge to the original savings deposited in the account.

Funds saved in a lifetime ISA can only be used to purchase a property costing £450,000 or less, which is bought with a mortgage. The property must not be bought until at least 12 months after the date on which the lifetime ISA was opened. Where a property is purchased jointly, all purchasers can use savings in a lifetime ISA and their government bonus to buy the property.

Consequently, a lifetime ISA should only be used for its intended purposes of saving for a first home or retirement; treating it as a short-term savings product may mean that the individual gets back less than what they put in. However, where used as intended, the government bonus makes it an attractive product, providing a significant return on savings.

Make Use Of A Lifetime ISA

Ellie opens a lifetime ISA aged 20, as she wishes to save for a deposit to buy her first home. She saves £4,000 a year for seven years, receiving a government bonus of £1,000 (25%) each year. After seven years, she has £35,000 (£28,000 savings plus £7,000 in government bonuses), plus accumulated interest in the account.

She withdraws the money to buy her first home, costing £250,000. The remainder of the purchase price is provided by a mortgage.

Making use of the lifetime ISA to save for a deposit has enabled Ellie to benefit from the government bonus and to enjoy the bonus and the accumulated interest tax-free.

11. Junior ISAs

Junior ISAs are long-term savings accounts for children. A child can have a Junior ISA if he or she is under 18, lives in the UK and does not have a child trust fund account.

The money in a Junior ISA belongs to the child, although anyone can put money in. There are two types of Junior ISA – cash Junior ISA and a stocks and shares Junior ISA. A child can have one or both, subject to the overall subscription limit. For 2022/23, the subscription limit for a Junior ISA is £9,000.

Income and gains in a Junior ISA are tax-free. Except in very limited circumstances, the money cannot be withdrawn until the child is 18. An ISA can be used to build up a nice savings pot for the child or maybe to fund university or college.

Once a child reaches 16, they can open an adult cash ISA and take advantage of the higher investment limits.

Junior ISAs
David invests £3,000 a year into a Junior ISA for his baby daughter Lucy. If he continues to invest £3,000 a year, when Lucy reaches 18, she will have a fund of £54,000 plus accumulated interest.
The interest is tax-free and is not taxed as David's income.

12. The Tax-Free Savings Band

There are various ways to receive tax-free interest on savings. In addition to the personal allowance and personal savings allowance (see Tip 7), depending on their other income, savers may also be able to benefit from the 0% starting rate on savings. Where the personal allowance and personal savings allowance are available, it is possible to enjoy savings income of up to £18,570 tax-free, in addition to interest on savings held in tax-free wrappers, such as ISAs. The tax-free limit of £18,570 for 2022/23 is made up of the personal allowance of £12,570, the personal savings allowance of £1,000 for basic rate taxpayers and the £5,000 nil rate band for savings income.

However, the starter savings rate band is not available to everyone. The starting rate applies to a maximum of £5,000 of non-dividend savings income. It is reduced by £1 for every £1 by which other taxable income exceeds the personal allowance, being extinguished once this reaches £5,000.

The Tax-Free Savings Band

Simon receives a salary of £14,000 and bank interest of £4,000 in 2022/23.

His salary of £14,000 exceeds his personal allowance for 2022/23 of £12,570 by £1,430. He, therefore, has taxable non-savings income of £1,430, which eats into the savings rate band of £5,000, thereby reducing it to £3,570 (£5,000 – £1,430).

Simon is a basic rate taxpayer. He is entitled to the personal savings allowance of £1,000, which shelters £1,000 of his bank interest from tax. The remaining £3,000 of his interest falls within his available starting savings rate band of £3,570, and as such, he enjoys the 0% starter rate on savings income within that band.

Consequently, Simon is able to enjoy the £4,000 of interest that he received in 2022/23 tax-free.

13. Using The Tax-Free Savings Band: Couples

For 2022/23, a tax rate of 0% applies to savings income falling within the savings band of £5,000 (see Tip 12). However, the special 0% savings rate is not available if the taxpayer has taxable non-savings income of more than £5,000.

Where available, the 0% band applies in addition to the personal savings allowance, set at £1,000 for basic rate taxpayers and £500 for higher rate taxpayers (see Tip 7).

Where spouses have significant savings income but minimal non-savings income, consider moving interest-earning accounts between spouses and civil partners to take advantage of the tax-free savings band available to each.

Using The Tax-Free Savings Band: Couples

Alfred and Freda are both retired. Alfred has a pension of £20,000 a year. He has also accumulated savings over the years, of £450,000 which generate gross interest of £4,500 a year.

Freda has a pension of £12,000 a year.

By transferring at least £350,000 of the savings (on which interest of £3,500 is received) into Freda's name, their savings income will be tax-free. The first £500 of their savings income will be covered by the remainder of Freda's personal allowance and the remaining £3,000 will fall within Freda's tax-free savings rate band.

Had all the savings income remained in Alfred's name, the interest in excess of his personal savings allowance of £1,000 would be taxed at 20%, generating a tax bill of £700 (£3,500 x 20%). As his taxable non-savings income of £7,430 (£20,000 – £12,570) exceeds £5,000, he does not benefit from the 0% savings rate. In Albert's hands, only the first £1,000 of the savings income, which is covered by his personal savings allowance, would be tax-free. Transferring the majority of his savings to Freda will save the tax of £700 that Alfred would have had to pay on the interest received in excess of his personal savings allowance.

It should be noted, however, that Albert should be comfortable with giving the majority of his savings to his wife – as always the tax tail should not wag the dog!

14. Equalising Savings Income To Save Tax

By equalising savings income, it is possible for a couple to receive savings income of up to £37,140 in addition to that held in tax-free wrappers, such as ISAs and dividends. For 2022/23, an individual may have a personal allowance of £12,570, a personal savings allowance of £1,000 if they are a basic rate taxpayer and a zero-rate savings band of £5,000 if this is not reduced by taxable non-savings income – a total of £18,570. However, if they have taxable non-savings income (such as a pension), this total may be reduced. A couple can each, in these circumstances, receive savings income of £18,570 – a combined total of £37,140

See also Tips 12 and 13.

To ensure that the opportunity to benefit from tax-free savings income is not wasted, couples should review their affairs to ensure that their savings are held so as to make the best possible use of the available allowances and zero-rate band.

Equalising Savings Income To Save Tax

Janet and David are both retired. Neither was born before 6 April 1935.

Janet has savings income of £40,000 in 2022/23. David has no income.

As she has only savings income, the first £18,570 (representing her personal allowance of £12,570, her personal savings allowance of £1,000 and her savings rate band of £5,000) is tax-free. The remaining £21,430 is taxed at 20%, generating a tax bill of £4,286.

However, if they put the income-generating investments in joint names (or transfer half to David), each will be treated as having savings income of £20,000. Both will benefit from the personal allowance of £12,570, the personal savings allowance of £1,000 and the savings band of £5,000, leaving them each with taxable savings income of £1,430 and a tax bill of £286. By equalising their savings income, their joint tax bill is £572 rather than £4,286, saving them £3,714 in tax.

15. Savings And A Mortgage? Consider Reducing Your Mortgage

If the interest rate on your mortgage is higher than the interest you earn on your savings, then you could save a considerable amount of money and reduce your tax bill on the interest received by using spare capital to pay off the mortgage on your own property. In the current climate of low interest rates where savings earn a very poor rate of return, this is likely to be worthwhile.

You could also save a considerable amount by switching to an offset mortgage if you feel the need to have the capital easily available should the need for it arise.

Remember that your mortgage payments are made from your after-tax income and hence cost you a lot more in total income to fund than you may think.

Savings And A Mortgage? Consider Reducing Your Mortgage

John has savings of £30,000 earning 1% per annum in interest, equal to £300. He is a higher rate taxpayer, and the interest received is covered by his personal savings allowance of £500, meaning he is able to enjoy it tax-free. He also has a mortgage of £30,000 on which he pays interest at a rate of 3.5%. This costs him £1,050 a year, which is payable from his after-tax income.

By paying off the mortgage, he no longer pays interest of £1,050 per annum on this; he also no longer receives the £300 in interest on his savings (which have been used to clear the mortgage). Overall, he will be £750 (£1,050 – £300) a year better off.

Funding the mortgage payments was using up £1,850 of John's gross income (which is equivalent to £1,050 after tax of 40% and National Insurance of 3.25% (£1,850 – (£1,850 x 43.25%) = £1,050)), which he could now use for other purposes, e.g. to increase his pension funding, which would save him further tax and increase his pension pot.

16. Utilise The Dividend Allowance

All taxpayers, regardless of the rate at which they pay tax, are entitled to a dividend allowance, set at £2,000 for 2022/23. Dividends covered by the allowance are taxed at a zero rate, although they still form part of the band earnings for the tax band in which the dividends (treated as the top slice of income) fall.

While utilising the dividend allowance may form part of the profit extraction strategy for family companies, ensuring that it is not wasted should also form part of an investment planning strategy. Where a taxpayer has savings which earn interest in excess of that which can be received tax-free, investing some of those savings in shares on which dividends will be paid can increase the taxpayer's tax-free investment income, as dividends up to the dividend allowance can be enjoyed tax-free.

Taxpayers are able to benefit from the dividend allowance in addition to any personal saving allowance to which they are entitled.

Utilise The Dividend Allowance

Tony is a higher rate taxpayer. He has a salary of £60,000 and also savings of £100,000 in a high interest account, which pays interest at the rate of 1.75%, earning Tony interest of £1,750 a year.

As he is a higher rate taxpayer, Tony is entitled to a personal savings allowance of £500. Consequently, the first £500 of his interest income is tax-free and he must pay tax at 40% on the balance of £1,250 – a tax bill of £500 (£1,250 x 40%).

After paying tax on his interest, Tony is left with £1,250.

After meeting with his financial adviser, Tony invests £72,000 in shares, leaving £28,000 in his savings account.

In 2022/23, he earns interest of £490 on his savings (£28,000 x 1.75%). He also receives dividends of £1,500.

The interest is tax-free as it is covered by the personal savings allowance (set at £500 for 2022/23) and the dividends are tax-free as they are covered by the dividend allowance (set at £2,000 for 2022/23). By swapping his investment mix to receive dividends and savings, he is able to enjoy all his investment income (totalling £1,990) tax-free.

Investing in shares opens up the possibility of receiving dividends of up to £2,000 tax-free, in addition to tax-free interest of £500.

A word of caution. When making investment decisions you should consider the return on investment and the associated risk as the value of shares can go down as well as up, and there is no guarantee that a dividend will be paid. You should also take into account any associated costs of changing the investment mix, as well as the tax savings, and ensure that the net result from making the switch is beneficial.

17. Pension Funding

Payments into a registered pension scheme attract tax relief at your highest rate of tax and are deemed to be paid net of basic rate tax. Contributions attract tax relief to the extent that they do not exceed 100% of earnings (or £3,600 if higher) and the available annual allowance.

The pension annual allowance is set at £40,000 for 2022/23 – the same level as for the previous three years. However, the allowance is reduced where both threshold income (broadly, income excluding pension contributions) is more than £200,000 and adjusted income (broadly, income including pension contributions (personal and employer)) is more than £240,000, by £1 for every £2 by which adjusted income exceeds £240,000 until the minimum allowance, set at £4,000 for 2022/23, is reached.

This means that the annual allowance for an individual who has both threshold income of more than £200,000 and adjusted income of more than £312,000 is £4,000 for 2022/23; at this level, the maximum reduction of £36,000 applies (1/2 (£312,000 – £240,000)). For 2019/20 and earlier years, the abatement applied where threshold income exceeded £110,000 and adjusted net income exceeded £150,000, with the allowance being reduced by £1 for every £2 by which adjusted net income exceeded £150,000, until the minimum allowance, set at £10,000, was reached. This must be taken into account when working out any brought forward allowances.

Unused allowances from the previous three tax years are carried into the current year, which means that it is possible to make significant tax-relieved contributions to a registered pension scheme. However, the current year's allowance must be fully utilised before using up allowances from previous years. Thus, for 2022/23, once contributions have been made up to the level of the 2022/23 allowance, contributions can be made to use, in order, brought forward allowances from 2019/20, 2020/21 and 2021/22. If unused allowances brought forward from 2019/20 are not used by 5 April 2023, they will be lost.

To prevent recycling of contributions, a reduced annual allowance (the Money Purchase Annual Allowance (MPAA)) applies where a person has, on reaching the age of 55, accessed pension savings in a money purchase (defined contribution) pension scheme. For 2022/23 the MPAA is set at £4,000.

The net cost to a basic rate taxpayer of a £100 contribution into a registered pension scheme is £80 (£100 less tax relief of £20). For higher rate taxpayers a £100 pension contribution costs £60, and for additional rate taxpayers the cost of a £100 pension contribution is just £55. This makes pension savings particularly tax-efficient.

The availability of the tax relief makes contributing to a pension worthwhile.

18. Making The Most Of The Pension Tax Annual Allowance

Tax relief on pension contributions is available on contributions up to the annual allowance. To the extent it is unused, the annual allowance can be carried forward for up to three years. However, the allowance for the current year must be used up before utilising allowances which have been carried forward.

The annual allowance is set at £40,000 for 2022/23 (and also for 2021/22, 2020/21 and 2019/20).

However, for 2022/23, 2021/22 and 2020/21, the annual allowance is reduced by £1 for every £2 where both threshold income exceeds £200,000 and adjusted income exceeds £240,000 until the minimum allowance, set at £4,000 for all of these years, is reached. For these years, a taxpayer will only receive the minimum allowance of £4,000 where both threshold income exceeds £200,000 and adjusted income exceeds £312,000 (see Tip 19).

However, for 2019/20, the abatement applied where both threshold income exceeded £110,000 and adjusted income exceeded £150,000, such that the annual allowance was reduced by £1 for every £2 for the excess of adjusted income over £150,000, until the minimum level of the allowance – set at £10,000 – was reached. For 2019/20, individuals with adjusted net income of £210,000 or more and threshold income of at least £110,000 would only receive the minimum annual allowance of £10,000.

Where income is sufficient, making higher levels of pension contributions to utilise unused annual allowances can be tax-efficient. For 2022/23, tax-relieved contributions can be made up to the level of the available allowance for 2022/23, plus any unused allowances brought forward from

2019/20, 2020/21 and 2021/22. The allowance for the current year is used first. Allowances brought forward from earlier years are used in chronological order. If unused allowances from 2019/20 are not used by 5 April 2023, they will be lost. Where allowances remain available from 2019/20, if funds permit consider making contributions equal to the available annual allowance for 2022/23 plus unused allowances from 2019/20 to make use of those allowances. Higher tax-relieved contributions can be made if unused allowances from 2020/21 and 2021/22 remain available.

It should be noted that a reduced annual allowance – the Money Purchase Annual Allowance (MPAA) – applies where a person has accessed pension savings in a money purchase (defined contribution) scheme on reaching the age of 55. This is set at £4,000 for 2022/23.

Employer contributions count towards the annual allowance.

It is important that tax-relieved contributions are not made in excess of the available annual allowances, as this will trigger an annual allowance charge designed to claw back the tax relief that was not actually due. Consideration also needs to be given to the lifetime allowance.

Making The Most Of The Pension Tax Annual Allowance

Paul has income of £120,000 in 2022/23. He has an annual allowance of £40,000 for 2022/23 and for each of the previous three years. In 2019/20, 2020/21 and 2021/22, he made pension contributions (gross) of £20,000, leaving £20,000 of his annual allowance unused in each of those years.

As Paul has inherited some money in 2022/23, he wishes to make a higher pension contribution in that year. The maximum tax-relieved contribution is capped at the lower of 100% of his earnings

(£120,000) and his available annual allowance. His available annual allowance for 2022/23 is £100,000, comprising his annual allowance for 2022/23 of £40,000 plus unused allowances from each of the previous three years of £20,000 per year.

Paul decides to make a pension contribution of £70,000 for 2022/23. This uses up his annual allowance of £40,000 for 2022/23 (the current year's allowance must be used before utilising unused allowances of the previous three years), £20,000 from 2019/20 and £10,000 from 2020/21. The unused allowances from an earlier year are used before those for a later year. After making the contribution, he has unused allowances of £10,000 for 2020/21 and £20,000 from 2021/22, which can be carried forward to 2023/24. Using the allowances brought forward from 2019/20 ensures that they are not wasted.

The contribution of £70,000 is paid net of basic rate tax (costing Paul £56,000). He claims higher rate relief (worth a further £14,000 (20% of £70,000)) through his self-assessment return. After tax-relief, Paul is able to enjoy a £70,000 pension contribution for £42,000, receiving tax relief of £28,000 (40% of £70,000).

19. Pension Contributions And High Earners

High earners with income in excess of £240,000 (including pension contributions) are subject to the annual allowance taper.

For 2022/23 the allowance is reduced where both threshold income (broadly, income excluding pension contributions) is more than £200,000 and adjusted income (broadly, income including pension contributions) is more than £240,000, by £1 for every £2 by which adjusted income exceeds £240,000 until the minimum allowance, set at £4,000 is reached. This means that for 2022/23, an individual who has both threshold income of more than £200,000 and adjusted income of more than £312,000 will only be entitled to an annual allowance of £4,000 as the maximum reduction of £36,000 applies (1/2 (£312,000 – £240,000)). The position is the same for 2021/22 and 2020/21.

For 2019/20, the allowance (set at £40,000) was reduced where both threshold income was more than £110,000 and adjusted income was more than £150,000 by £1 for every £2 by which adjusted income exceeded £150,000 until the minimum allowance, set at £10,000, was reached. Thus, an individual who had both threshold income of more than £110,000 and adjusted income of more than £210,000 in 2019/20 was only entitled to an annual allowance of £10,000 as the maximum reduction of £30,000 applied (1/2 (£210,000 – £150,000)).

When dealing with unused allowances from earlier years, it is important that the correct abatement thresholds are used.

Note that the taper only applies if both the threshold income and the adjusted income thresholds are exceeded. If threshold income is less than £200,000 for 2022/23, 2021/22 or 2020/21, the allowance is not reduced, even if adjusted income is more than £240,000. For 2019/20, the equivalent figure was £110,000.

The adjusted income figure includes pension contributions made by both the individual and the employer. However, personal pension contributions are deducted in arriving at threshold income. Thus, it may be possible to make personal pension contributions to reduce threshold income below £200,000, thereby preventing the taper from applying.

Pension Contributions And High Earners

John has a salary of £205,000 for 2022/23.

He has unused annual allowance of £40,000 brought forward from 2021/22. He has used his annual allowance in full for 2020/21 and 2019/20.

His employer wishes to make a pension contribution of £75,000.

Without taking any action, John's adjusted income would be £280,000 (£205,000 plus the planned employer pension contribution of £75,000). As his threshold income is £205,000, and his adjusted income is £280,000 the taper would apply and John's pension annual allowance for 2022/23 would be reduced to £20,000 (£40,000 – (1/2 (£280,000 – £240,000))). This would leave him with available annual allowances of £60,000 – the reduced allowance of £20,000 for 2022/23 and the allowance of £40,000 brought forward from 2021/22. This is not sufficient to cover the planned employer contribution of £75,000.

However, if John makes a personal contribution of £5,000, his threshold income is reduced to £200,000. As threshold income does not exceed £200,000, the taper of the allowance does not apply.

Consequently, the full annual allowance of £40,000 is available for

2022/23, meaning he has annual allowances of £80,000 (£40,000 for 2022/23 and £40,000 unused in 2021/22) available to him in 2022/23. This is sufficient to shelter both the planned employer contribution of £75,000 and his personal contribution of £5,000 (£80,000 in total), utilising all his available annual allowances.

20. Making Pension Contributions For Family Members

Most people are unaware that the government allows annual contributions of up to £3,600 gross (£2,880 net of basic rate tax) to be made into a registered pension scheme, regardless of your level of income or age.

So, if you wish, you can contribute into a pension scheme for your non-working spouse, children, etc. The contribution is deemed to be made net of basic rate tax, even if they are non-taxpayers. Consequently, a pension contribution of £3,600 will only cost you £2,880.

This can be useful in a family company situation when looking to extract profits in a tax-efficient manner.

Making Pension Contributions For Family Members

John wishes to increase his family's pension fund at retirement and makes a contribution of £2,880 into his non-working wife's pension fund. This is worth £3,600 in the scheme and he is able to obtain a tax saving of £720 by doing so.

He also contributes £2,880 into each of his three children's pension schemes, which again is worth £3,600 in each of their schemes, receiving a further £720 tax advantage in each scheme (£2,160 in total).

Starting pension contributions for his children at a young age will mean that they will have a considerably bigger pension fund at retirement than, say, someone starting their pension funding in their thirties.

21. Invest In A Venture Capital Trust (VCT)

If your attitude to investment risk is at the higher end of the scale, then you could invest in a Venture Capital Trust (VCT). These are designed to encourage investment into smaller higher-risk trading companies.

Venture capital trusts offer significant tax benefits in return for the risk.

Income tax relief is available at 30% for the tax year in which the subscription was made (up to a maximum subscription of £200,000 per tax year).

Dividends on VCT shares are received free of tax.

Relief from capital gains tax is available on disposals of VCT shares.

Invest In A Venture Capital Trust (VCT)
Peter invests £10,000 into a VCT.
He receives income tax relief of £3,000 (£10,000 x 30%).
Any dividends that are received on his VCT shares can be enjoyed tax-free.

22. Invest In An Enterprise Investment Scheme (EIS)

Individuals who are happy to take an element of risk in return for the opportunity to benefit from tax relief on their investment may consider investing in one of the venture capital schemes.

The Enterprise Investment Scheme (EIS) is designed to help smaller higher-risk companies raise finance by offering a range of tax reliefs to investors.

Under the EIS, tax relief is available to individuals who subscribe for shares in an EIS company. Income tax relief is given at a rate of 30% on the cost of the shares, subject to a maximum investment of £1 million per year (or £2 million per person per year where the excess over £1 million is invested in knowledge-intensive companies). The shares must be fully paid up. The income tax relief is, therefore, worth up to £300,000 to the investor (or up to £600,000 where the investment is in a knowledge-intensive company). The investor can also benefit from capital gains tax and loss reliefs.

Income tax relief is normally given for the tax year for which the investment is made. However, the investor can choose to treat some or all of the shares as issued in the previous tax year and claim relief for that year, although it should be noted that if the shares are sold within three years of the date of issue, income tax relief will be wholly or partly withdrawn.

EIS shares may also qualify for capital gains tax reliefs.

Disposal relief is available as long as the shares are held for at least three years before the date of disposal and income tax relief has been received on the full subscription and not withdrawn. Where disposal relief is available, no capital gains tax is payable on any gain made on disposal.

Where an asset is sold and the proceeds are invested in EIS shares, any gain on the sale of the asset can be deferred by claiming deferral relief on all or part of the gain. To qualify, the investor must subscribe for EIS shares in the period starting from 12 months before the disposal of the asset to 36 months after. The gain when the EIS shares are sold or cease to be eligible shares (for example, if the company no longer meets the definition of a qualifying company).

A loss on the sale of the shares can be set against any chargeable gains; it may also be possible to set the loss against income tax.

There is no tax relief for dividends paid on EIS shares, which are taxed according to the normal dividend tax rules.

Note: restrictions apply where an individual investor is connected with the EIS company. This is the case where he or she is remunerated as an employee or director or owns (or is entitled to possess) 30% of the ordinary share capital, 30% of the voting rights or 30% of the assets in a winding up of either the EIS company or a subsidiary of that company.

Invest In An Enterprise Investment Scheme (EIS)

Harry sells some shares in 2021/22 for £500,000, realising a gain of £90,000. He invests the proceeds in an EIS company in 2022/23. The investment qualifies for EIS relief, allowing Harry to benefit from income tax relief of £150,000 (£500,000 x 30%). He elects to treat 50% of the investment as having been made in 2021/22 and the remaining 50% in 2022/23, claiming income tax relief of £75,000 for each year.

Harry also elects to claim deferral relief in respect of £77,700 of the gains on the shares that were sold to fund the EIS investment. The non-deferred gain of £12,300 is sheltered by his annual exempt amount for 2022/23 (set at £12,300).

As long as he keeps the EIS shares for at least three years, he will benefit from the full income tax relief and will not pay capital gains tax on the sale of the EIS shares. However, the deferred gain of £77,700 will crystallise when the EIS shares are sold.

23. Invest In A Seed Enterprise Investment Scheme (SEIS)

The Seed Enterprise Investment Scheme (SEIS) is designed to help small, early-stage companies to raise equity finance by offering tax reliefs to investors who purchase new shares in a company within the scheme and who have no more than a 30% stake in those companies.

Income tax relief is available to investors who subscribe for shares in a qualifying SEIS company. Shares must be held for three years. Tax relief is given at a rate of 50%. The maximum annual investment is £100,000. Relief is not available if the investor is connected with the company.

Capital gains tax relief is available where gains are reinvested in qualifying SEIS shares. Relief is available for 50% of the reinvested gains. The relief is subject to the £100,000 investment cap.

Invest In A Seed Enterprise Investment Scheme (SEIS)

Toby realises chargeable gains of £100,000 from the sale of a residential property, which he reinvests in shares in a SEIS scheme.

Toby is an additional rate taxpayer and has utilised his capital gains tax annual exempt amount elsewhere.

He receives capital gains tax relief on 50% of the amount reinvested (£50,000), on which he saves capital gains tax of £14,000 (£50,000 x 28%).

He also receives income tax relief of 50% on his investment of £100,000, saving a further £50,000 in tax.

Chapter 3:
Family Companies

24. Pay A Small Salary To Retain State Pension Entitlement

Where a business is run as a company, funds will need to be extracted for personal use. It makes sense to do this in a tax-efficient manner.

When looking to extract funds from a personal or family company, consideration should be given to paying a small salary to preserve entitlement to the state pension and contributory benefits.

Where a person's earnings fall between the lower earnings limit for Class 1 National Insurance purposes (£123 per week for 2022/23) and the primary earnings threshold (£190 per week from 6 April 2022 to 5 July 2022 and £242 per week from 6 July 2022 to 5 April 2023) – equivalent to an annual salary of between £6,396 and £11,908– they are deemed to have paid National Insurance contributions at a notional zero rate.

This will ensure that the year is a qualifying year for state pension and benefits purposes, without having to actually pay any primary National Insurance contributions.

However, as the primary threshold and the secondary threshold are not aligned for 2022/23, it should be noted that unless the employment allowance is available or the individual is under 21, an apprentice under the age of 25, an armed forces veteran in the first year of their first civilian employment since leaving the armed forces or a new Freeport employee, employer's National Insurance contributions will be payable to the extent that the salary exceeds the secondary threshold, set at £175 per week (£9,100 per year) for 2022/23.

For 2022/23, employer's National Insurance contributions are payable at the rate of 15.05%. The rate is increased from 13.8% to 15.05% for 2022/23 only pending the introduction of the Health and Social Care Levy from 6

April 2023.

It should be noted that directors have an annual earnings period for National Insurance purposes, meaning the annual limits should be applied rather than the weekly or monthly equivalents, regardless of the director's actual pay interval. The annual primary threshold for directors for 2022/23 is £11,908 (equivalent to £229 per week).

The benefit of paying a salary of at least £6,396 for the year is that it ensures that the year is a qualifying year which helps secure entitlement to the state pension and certain contributory benefits, without actually costing the director anything. A person needs 35 qualifying years to qualify for the full single-tier state pension and a minimum of ten qualifying years to receive a reduced state pension.

Extracting some profits in the form of a salary is also beneficial from a tax perspective. See Tip 25.

For 2022/23, a salary of between the lower earnings limit of £6,396 and secondary threshold of £9,100 per annum (£533 and £758 per month) can be paid without triggering a liability to either employee or employer Class 1 National Insurance contributions, whilst ensuring that the year is also a qualifying year for National Insurance purposes.

However, paying a higher salary can be tax-efficient, even if this means that some secondary contributions are payable. See Tip 25.

Pay A Small Salary To Retain State Pension Entitlement

Oliver is a director and 100% shareholder in his personal company. In 2022/23, he pays himself a salary of £8,000 to maintain his contribution record and to preserve his entitlement to the state pension and contributory benefits. This can be paid free of employer's and employee's National Insurance contributions and, as long as £8,000 of his personal allowance is available, free of tax.

He extracts further profits from the company in the form of dividends.

25. Optimal Salary Where NIC Employment Allowance Is Not Available

The optimal salary level depends on whether the National Insurance employment allowance is available to shelter any employer's National Insurance liability that would arise on the payment of the salary.

The NIC employment allowance is not available where the sole employee is also a director. This is usually the case for a personal company.

Where the employment allowance is not available and the director is over the age of 21 (and none of the other upper secondary thresholds for employers apply), for 2022/23, the optimal salary (assuming the personal allowance is not used elsewhere) is equal to the primary threshold. For 2022/23, the primary threshold is set at £190 per week (£823 per month) for the period from 6 April 2022 to 5 July 2022 and at £242 per week (£1,048 per month) for the period from 6 July 2022 to 5 April 2023. The annualised primary threshold is £11,908 for 2022/23. It should be remembered that directors have an annual earnings period for National Insurance purposes.

Although the maximum salary that can be paid without having to pay any National Insurance (employer's or employee's) is £9,100 – equal to the secondary threshold – the fact that the salary and employer's National Insurance are deductible for corporation tax makes it worthwhile paying a salary equal to the annualised primary threshold of £11,908 and paying employer's National Insurance at 15.05% to the extent that the salary exceeds £11,908. The corporation tax deduction at 19% outweighs the National Insurance cost on the higher salary at 15.05%.

However, once the salary level reaches the primary threshold of £11,908, a liability to employee's National Insurance contributions arises, so that employee contributions of 13.25% are payable to the extent that the salary exceeds £11,908, as well as employer contributions of 15.05%. Employer's National Insurance contributions are deductible for corporation tax, meaning the effective rate after allowing for corporation tax relief is 12.19% (15.05% − (15.05% @ 19%)). The combined NIC hit on the excess above £11.908is more than the corporation tax relief of 19% on the salary and employer's National Insurance contributions, so it is not efficient to pay a salary of more than £11,908 for 2022/23 (unless the employment allowance is available (for which see Tip 26) or the director is under the age of 21 or another upper secondary threshold for employers applies).

There is some administration involved in paying the employer's National Insurance over to HMRC. Consequently, the decision may be made to forgo the small savings achieved by paying a salary of £9,880 and instead pay a salary of £9,100, which can be paid free of any National Insurance, to save the associated administration. However, the administration burden can be minimised by having an annual PAYE scheme.

It should be noted that the rates of primary and secondary Class 1 National Insurance contributions are increased by 1.25% for 2022/23 only pending the introduction of the Health and Social Care Levy. Consequently, the main primary rate is 13.25%, the additional primary rate is 3.25% and the secondary rate is 15.05% for 2022/23 only. The rates are due to revert to, respectively, 12%, 2% and 13.8% from 6 April 2023 when the Health and Social Care Levy comes into effect. However, employees and employers will also be required to pay the Health and Social Care Levy of 1.25% of earnings liable to Class 1 National Insurance contributions from this date.

Looking ahead, from 1 April 2023 the corporation tax regime is reformed and where profits are higher than the lower limit (£50,000 as divided by the number of associated companies plus one), corporation tax will be payable at a rate higher than the current rate of 19%. Where profits exceed the upper limit (£250,000 divided by the number of associated companies plus one), corporation tax will be payable at the rate of 25%. The rate at which corporation tax is paid will affect the calculation of the optimal salary level.

Optimal Salary Where NIC Employment Allowance Is Not Available

Helga is the director and sole employee of her personal company. As such her company is not entitled to claim the employment allowance. She is aged 42.

She wants to pay a salary for 2022/23 which is sufficient to ensure that the year is a qualifying year for state pension purposes and wants to know the level at which she should set her salary. For the year to be a qualifying year, she must pay a salary of at least £6,396 for 2022/23.

However, she can increase the salary that she pays herself to £9,100 (the level of the secondary threshold for 2022/23) before any National Insurance is due. It will be beneficial to pay a salary equal to the primary threshold for 2022/23 of £11,908, as while paying an additional 0 to increase the salary to £11,908 will incur an employer's National Insurance liability of £422.60 (£2,808 @ 15.05%), the additional salary and associated National Insurance of £3,230.60 (£2,808 + 422.60) is deductible for corporation tax purposes, reducing the corporation tax bill by £613.81 (£3,230.6 @ 19%) – a net tax saving of £191.21 (£613.81 - £422.60)).

Once the salary exceeds the annual primary threshold of £11,908, employee National Insurance is also payable at 13.25%, meaning that paying a salary in excess of this is not worthwhile as the National Insurance (employee's and employer's) on the additional salary outweighs the corporation tax saving on the salary and employer's National Insurance at 19%.

26. Pay A Higher Salary Where The NIC Employment Allowance Is Available

Eligible employers are able to claim an employment allowance which reduces the amount of secondary employer's NIC that they pay. For 2022/23, the allowance is set at £5,000 (capped at the secondary Class 1 National Insurance bill for the year where this is lower).

The employment allowance is not available to companies where the sole employee is also a director. Thus, while family companies may be able to benefit from the allowance as long as they have more than one employee (or where they only have one employee, that employee is not also the director), the employment allowance will not be available to a typical one-man company where the director is the sole employee.

In a company where the employment allowance is available and would otherwise be wasted, it is possible to make further savings by paying a salary at a level which is above the primary threshold. As long as the personal allowance is available in full to set against the salary and the unused employment allowance is sufficient to shelter the salary in excess of the secondary threshold up to the level of the personal allowance, the optimal salary is one equal to the personal allowance. For 2022/23, this is equivalent to a salary of £12,570.

The additional salary in excess of the primary threshold is deductible for corporation tax purposes, saving corporation tax at 19%. Although paying a salary above the primary NIC threshold will mean that the employee will suffer Class 1 NICs on the excess at 13.25%, this is more than offset by the corporation tax saving (at 19%) on the additional salary. As the employment allowance is available, no employer's Class 1 National Insurance is payable.

As long as the salary does not exceed the personal allowance (£12,570 for

2022/23) and the personal allowance is not utilised elsewhere, there is no income tax to pay either.

However, it is not worth paying a salary in excess of the personal allowance, as the tax and employee's National Insurance hit at 33.25% is more than the corporation tax saving of 19% on the additional salary.

It should be noted that the employment allowance is not available for 2022/23 where the company's Class 1 National Insurance bill for 2021/22 is £100,000 or more.

Where the employment allowance is available, there is some administration involved in paying the employee's National Insurance over to HMRC. However, where the recipient is a director and the annual earnings period is used rather than the alternative arrangements, if the director is paid a monthly salary of £1,047.50, the employee's NIC will all be paid in months 10, 11 and 12.

Pay A Higher Salary Where The NIC Employment Allowance Is Available

Sophie is the director of her family company. Her daughter Jessica also works in the business. Jessica is under 21 and the employment allowance is available in full.

As Jessica is under the age of 21, no employer's NIC is payable until her earnings exceed the upper secondary threshold for under 21s (set at £50,270 for 2022/23). Employee contributions are payable as for other employees.

For 2022/23 Sophie is paid a salary of £12,570. In the absence of the NIC employment allowance, the company would pay employer NIC of £522.24 ((£12,570 − £9,100) @ 15.05%).

However, as this is covered by the NIC employment allowance, no actual employer's NIC is payable. Sophie will pay employee's NIC of £87.72 to the extent that the salary of £12,570 exceeds the primary threshold of £11,908 for 2022/23 (£662 @ 13.25%). No income tax is payable as her salary is covered by her personal allowance.

Salary payments are deductible for corporation tax purposes. Paying a salary of £12,570 rather than one of £9,880 will generate an additional corporation tax deduction of £125.78 (£662 @ 19%). This outweighs the employee NIC of £87.72 payable on the higher salary, meaning that overall Sophie is £38.06 (£511.10 – £356.43) better off by paying herself a salary of £12,570 rather than one of £9,880.

If she pays a salary in excess of the personal allowance, the additional salary over the personal allowance will be taxable and the income tax payable, combined with employee's NIC, will outweigh any corporation tax deduction. The optimal salary where the employment allowance is available is one equal to the personal allowance, set at £12,570 for 2022/23.

27. Extraction Of Profits In A Tax-Efficient Manner

There are various ways in which profits can be extracted from a personal or family company and consideration should be given to formulating a tax-efficient extraction policy. As circumstances vary, there is no substitute for crunching the numbers and it is advisable to take professional advice.

A popular and effective strategy is to pay a small salary of at least the lower earnings limit (£123 per week for 2022/23 (£6,396 per year)).

For 2022/23, the primary and secondary thresholds are not aligned, but as shown in Tip 25, it is more tax-efficient to pay a salary equal to the annual primary threshold of £11,908 rather than one equal to the secondary threshold of £9,100, despite the fact that some employer's National Insurance is payable because of the corporation tax relief at 19% that is available on the salary and the employer's National Insurance. Where the recipient is not a director, the thresholds applying at the time that the payment is made should be used. The primary threshold is £190 per week (£823 per month) for the period from 6 April 2022 to 5 July 2022 and £242 per week (£1,048 per month) for the period from 6 July 2022 to 5 April 2023.

Where the employment allowance is available, it is tax-efficient to pay a higher salary, equal to the personal allowance (see Tip 26). For 2022/23, this is equal to a salary of £12,570.

Once a salary at the optimal level has been paid, it is generally more tax-efficient to extract further profits as dividends. This is generally more tax-efficient than paying a salary or bonus as although there is no corporation tax deduction for dividends, also no National Insurance contributions are due on dividends; the dividend savings outweigh the lack of a corporation tax deduction.

All taxpayers, regardless of the rate at which they pay tax, are entitled to an annual dividend allowance of £2,000. The allowance means that the first £2,000 of dividend income (treated as the top slice of income) is taxed at a zero rate. Once the allowance and any remaining personal allowance have been used up, dividends are taxed at the lower dividend rates of tax, which for 2022/23 are set at 8.75% to the extent that they fall within the basic rate band, 33.75% to the extent that they fall within the higher rate band and 39.35% to the extent that they fall within the additional rate band. The dividend allowance forms part of the tax band in which the dividends fall. The rates at which dividends are taxed were increased by 1.25% from 6 April 2022 to provide funding for health and adult social care.

Note: dividends are paid from after-tax profits and must be properly declared in accordance with company law. They can only be paid if the company has sufficient retained profits. In addition, they must be paid in proportion to shareholdings.

Extraction Of Profits In A Tax-Efficient Manner

Olly is the sole shareholder and director of OB Ltd and the only employee. For 2022/23, he pays himself a salary of £11,908 for the year.

As the employment allowance is not available, this is the optimal salary (see Tip 25). After paying the salary, OB Ltd has profits before tax of £12,000, which Olly wants to withdraw as a salary or a dividend.

Olly has £662 (£12,570 − £11,908) of his personal allowance available, which can be set against any salary or dividends that he receives. If Olly extracts the remaining profits as a salary or bonus,

OB Ltd will need to pay employer's National Insurance. After allowing for employer's National Insurance, OB Ltd has £10,430 (£12,000 – (£12,000 x 15.05/115.05)) available to pay as a salary. Olly has £662 of his personal allowance available (£12,570 – £11,908). On the additional salary of £10,430 Olly will pay income tax of £1,953.60 ((£10,430 – £662) @ 20%) and employee's National Insurance of £1,381.98 (£10,430 @ 13.25%) – a total of £3,335.58.58, leaving him with £7,094.42 (£10,430 – £3,335,58) in his pocket.

Dividends are paid out of post-tax profits. The pre-tax profits of £12,000 are equivalent to post-tax profits of £9,720 after deducting corporation tax at 19% (£12,000 – (£12,000 @ 19%)).

The dividends of £9,720 are set against the remaining personal allowance of £662 and the dividend allowance of £2,000. The remaining dividends of £7,058 are taxed at 8.75%, a tax bill of £617.58. Olly, therefore, retains profits of £9,102.42 (£9,720 – £617.58) by taking the dividend route. By taking dividends he retains £2008 more of the profits than if he had extracted them in the form of further salary or a bonus.

28. Dividend Allowance For All

All taxpayers, regardless of the rate at which they pay tax, are entitled to the dividend allowance, set at £2,000 for 2022/23. This provides the opportunity to extract further profits by making family members shareholders and paying them dividends (and where unused) utilising their basic rate band.

However, remember, dividends must be paid in proportion to shareholdings and can only be paid from retained earnings. See Tip 29 for the use of an alphabet share structure, which provides the facility to tailor dividends to the circumstances of the recipient.

Dividend Allowance For All

Matthew is the director of a family company in which his wife and their three grown-up daughters are also shareholders. They each own 20% of the ordinary share capital in the company, with rights to 20% of the distributable profits and assets in a winding up. His wife and daughters all work and their personal allowance is set against their salaries.

Matthew pays himself a salary of £11,908. He has rental income of £7,000 which utilises the remainder of his personal allowance.

Further profits of £10,000 (post-tax) are extracted by way of dividends, with Matthew, his wife, and their daughters all receiving a dividend of £2,000 each. None of them receives dividends from other sources. The dividends from the family company are sheltered by the dividend allowance and are received tax-free.

This can be compared to the position that would have arisen had Matthew been the sole shareholder and received a dividend of £10,000. The first £2,000 would have been covered by the dividend allowance, but the remaining £8,000 would have been taxed at the lower dividend rate of 8.75%, generating a tax bill of £700.

Paying dividends to other family members and making use of their dividend allowance saves the family tax of £700.

29. Use An Alphabet Share Structure To Tailor Dividends

Under company law requirements, not only must a company have sufficient retained profits in order to pay dividends, but it must also pay dividends in proportion to shareholdings. This means that if two shareholders have the same number of the same class of shares, they must receive the same dividend. This requirement restricts the ability to pay dividends in a tax-efficient manner by tailoring the amount paid so as to utilise available dividend allowances and basic rate bands.

However, the restriction can be overcome by having an 'alphabet' share structure whereby one shareholder holds 'A' Class ordinary shares, another 'B' Class ordinary shares, another 'C' Class ordinary shares, and so on. By having alphabet shares, it is possible to declare different dividends for each class of shareholder, thereby tailoring the dividend to the circumstances of the shareholder and extracting profits from the family company in a tax-efficient manner.

Use An Alphabet Share Structure To Tailor Dividends

Harry is a director of a family company, as is his wife Isabelle. Harry is a higher rate taxpayer. Isabelle is a stay-at-home parent. She has no other income.

The company has post-tax profits of £40,000, which they wish to extract in 2022/23 in the form of dividends.

If Harry and Isabelle each own 50% of the ordinary share capital of the company, they would each receive a dividend of £20,000. After utilising his dividend allowance of £2,000, Harry would be taxed on his remaining dividends of £18,000 at the dividend upper rate of 33.75%, generating a tax bill of £6,075. Isabelle has both her personal allowance of £12,570 and her dividend allowance of £2,000 available, allowing her to receive £14,570 of dividends tax-free. The remaining £5,430 is taxed at the dividend ordinary rate of 8.75%, generating a tax bill of £475.12. The couple's combined tax bill would be £6,550.12.

If, instead, they used an alphabet share structure, such that Harry owned one A ordinary share and Isabelle owned one B ordinary share, it would be possible to lower their combined tax bill by declaring different dividends for A and B Class shareholders. By declaring a dividend of £2,000 per share for A Class holders, Harry would receive a dividend of £2,000, which would be covered by his dividend allowance with the result that no tax would be payable by Harry. To extract the remaining post-tax profits of £38,000, a dividend of £38,000 per share could be declared for B Class shareholders. Isabelle would be able to set her personal allowance of £12,570 and her dividend allowance of £2,000 against the shares, receiving dividends of £14,570 tax-free. The dividend allowance uses up £2,000 of her basic rate band, leaving £35,700 available. The remaining dividend of £23,430 (£38,000 – £14,570) would fall entirely in her basic rate band, being taxed at 8.75% (a tax bill of £2,050.12).

By adopting an alphabet share structure and tailoring the dividend payments, Harry and Isabelle will pay £4,500 less in tax on the total dividend payment of £40,000. This is achieved by moving the tax liability on £18,000 of dividends from the upper dividend rate of 33.75% to the ordinary dividend rate of 8.75%, reducing the tax rate on those dividends by 25% in the process.

30. Timing Of Bonus Payments To Delay Tax

Due to the way the tax rules work, it is possible to have a deduction for a bonus declared in a set of company accounts and pay the bonus up to nine months after the year-end.

The payment of the bonus could be timed to fall in a different tax year where other income is lower and this would result in a lower tax liability. Alternatively, delaying paying the bonus may defer the time at which the tax is payable.

Timing Of Bonus Payments To Delay Tax

Jane is preparing the company accounts for J Ltd, her own limited company.

The company's year-end is 31 December 2021. J Ltd declares a bonus of £10,000 to Jane for the year to 31 December 2021 and makes provision in the accounts. The bonus is due for payment and actually paid in August 2022.

Jane is a higher rate taxpayer in 2021/22 and a basic rate taxpayer in 2022/23.

As the bonus is paid within nine months of the company year-end, a deduction is permitted for corporation tax purposes in the company accounts for the year to 31 December 2021.

However, the bonus is taxed for PAYE purposes when it is paid in August 2022. Thus, as the bonus is paid in August 2022, falling in the 2022/23 tax year, Jane pays tax at the basic rate on the bonus. Had the bonus been paid in December 2021 it would have been taxed in 2021/22 and Jane would have paid tax on the bonus at the higher rate. Delaying the payment of the bonus halves Jane's personal tax bill without adversely affecting the corporation tax deduction. While the associated National Insurance is slightly higher due to the rates for 2022/23 being 1.25% higher than in 2021/22, overall, the combined bill is lower by delaying the payment.

31. Make Use Of Loans To Directors

Used wisely, loans from a family company to a director can be a cheap source of temporary finance. As long as the loan is paid back within nine months and one day of the end of the accounting period in which it was made, there is no tax to pay on the loan, other than any benefit-in-kind charge that will arise if the loan is not classed as a small loan. This will be the case where the outstanding loan balance exceeds £10,000 at any point in the tax year. These rules allow the director to make use of the money tax-free (or virtually tax-free) for up to 21 months.

Under the loans to participators rules, a 'section 455' tax charge applies to any loan balance which remains outstanding at the corporation tax due date (nine months and one day after the end of the accounting period) which must be paid over to HMRC. The rate of section 455 tax is aligned with the dividend upper rate. Consequently, the rate is 32.5% where the loan was made before 6 April 2022 and 33.75% where the loan was made on or after 6 April 2022.

Section 455 tax is a temporary tax which is refunded once the loan is cleared. The refunded section 455 tax is set against the corporation tax liability for the accounting period in which the loan is repaid. If there is no corporation tax liability for that period, it can be repaid nine months and one day after the end of the accounting period in which the loan was repaid.

It is possible to avoid the section 455 tax charge by repaying the loan before the corporation tax due date, but care must be taken not to fall foul of either the 30-day rule (which renders repayment of £5,000 or more ineffective if the funds are re-borrowed within 30 days) or the intentions and arrangements rule (under which repayments of £15,000 or more are deemed ineffective if arrangements exist to re-borrow the funds at the time that the repayment is made).

The loan can be repaid by introducing funds into the company or crediting dividend, salary or bonus payments to the director's loan account to clear the overdrawn balance.

However, as illustrated by Tip 32, clearing the loan will not always be the most tax-efficient option.

Make Use Of Loans To Directors

Matt is the director of his family company, which is close. The company prepares accounts to 31 March each year. During the year to 31 March 2023, Matt needs to borrow £8,000 to do some work on the family home. He borrows the funds from the company on 6 April 2022. The loan is cleared by a dividend which is declared on 30 December 2023.

As the loan balance is less than £10,000 throughout, there is no benefit-in-kind to pay on the loan or any Class 1A NIC. The loan is repaid by 1 January 2024 (the due date for corporation tax for the year to 31 March 2023), so there is no tax to pay under the loans to participators rules.

Matt is able to enjoy the use of the money tax-free for nearly 21 months – much cheaper than a bank loan.

32. Leave A Loan To A Director Outstanding And Pay Section 455 Tax

If a director has an overdrawn loan account at the end of the accounting period, clearing that balance before the date on which corporation tax for the period becomes due will prevent a section 455 tax charge from arising (see Tip 31). However, it should not be assumed that clearing the loan is always the most tax-efficient option – depending on the circumstances it may be preferable to leave the loan outstanding and take the section 455 hit, especially if the loan can be cleared more tax-efficiently in a later tax year.

Paying a dividend or bonus to clear the loan will have its own tax implications. A dividend is paid out of post-tax profits, so the company will need pre-tax profits of £1,235 for every £1,000 paid out as a dividend to allow for corporation tax at 19%. Further, once the dividend allowance has been used up, the dividend will be taxable in the hands of the recipient. For 2022/23, dividends are taxed at 8.75% where the director is a basic rate taxpayer, at 33.75% where the director is a higher rate taxpayer and at 39.35% where the director is an additional rate taxpayer. The tax paid on the dividend will not be recovered, unlike the section 455 tax.

The company will need to pay a dividend that is sufficient to both clear the loan and also to pay the associated tax on that dividend (unless the director has sufficient funds outside the company to meet the tax bill). Likewise, if the loan is cleared by paying a bonus, there will be employer's National Insurance to pay by the company. The bonus will also be taxable in the hands of the director and liable to employee's National Insurance.

If the director is a higher rate taxpayer, for 2022/23 this will be a hit of 43.25% (40% income tax and 3.25% employee's National Insurance) – more than the section 455 charge. The company will also pay employer's National

Insurance at 15.05% for 2022/23. If paying a bonus to clear the outstanding loan, the bonus will need to be sufficient to clear the loan and pay the associated tax and employee's National Insurance.

Consequently, it is important to look at the overall picture in determining whether it is better to clear the overdrawn director's loan account or pay the section 455 charge.

Leave A Loan To A Director Outstanding And Pay Section 455 Tax

Gary is the director of his personal company, G Ltd. He prepares accounts to 31 December each year. At 31 December 2022, his director's account is overdrawn by £20,000.

Gary is a higher rate taxpayer. He has already used his dividend allowance for 2022/23. He is planning to sell a property in May 2024, which will release sufficient funds to clear the loan. If the account remains overdrawn on 1 October 2023 (the due date for corporation tax for the year to 31 December 2022), the company will need to pay section 455 tax on the outstanding loan balance of £6,750 (£20,000 @ 33.75%).

If the company pays a dividend to Gary, he will pay tax at 33.75% on that dividend. To ensure that Gary has sufficient funds to clear the loan and pay the associated tax on the dividend, the company will need to pay Gary a dividend of £30,189. He will pay tax of £10,189 (£30,189 @ 33.75%) on the dividend, leaving him with £20,000 to clear the loan. The tax paid by Gary on the dividend declared to clear the loan is more than the section 455 tax.

Similarly, if Gary is paid a bonus, he will need to receive a bonus of £35,242 to have sufficient funds to clear the £20,000 loan. He will pay tax of £14,097 and employee's National Insurance of £1,145. The company will also pay employer's National Insurance of £5,304 (£35,242 @ 15.05%).

By contrast, if the company leaves the account overdrawn, the only tax payable will be the section 455 tax of £6,750. If Gary clears the loan in May 2024 (which falls in the year to 31 December 2024), the section 455 tax will be refundable on 1 October 2025 and can be set against the corporation tax liability for the year to 31 December 2024, meaning that the section 455 tax paid is only a temporary loan to HMRC.

33. Choose Which Loans To Repay

The rate of section 455 tax is aligned with the dividend higher rate. For loans made on or after 6 April 2022, section 455 tax is payable at the rate of 33.75%. The rate is 32.5% for loans made on or after 6 April 2016 and before 6 April 2022. Section 455 tax was charged at the rate of 25% on outstanding loans made prior to 6 April 2016.

Where a director has a number of outstanding loans on which section 455 tax has been paid, the rate at which the tax was paid may not be the same for each of the loans. As section 455 tax is a temporary tax which is repaid nine months and one day after the end of the accounting period in which the loan was cleared, to maximise the tax repayment, it make sense to clear the loans which have suffered the highest rate of section 455 tax first. There is no requirement to clear earlier loans before clearing later loans.

To maximise the tax repayment, loans should be cleared in the following order:

1.   Loans made on or after 6 April 2022 on which section 455 tax has not yet been paid. This will save section 455 tax on the loan at 33.75%.
2.   Loans made on or after 6 April 2022 on which section 455 tax has been paid. This will generate a repayment of 33.75% of the amount repaid.
3.   Loans made on or after 6 April 2016 and before 6 April 2022. Loans on which section 455 tax has yet to be paid should be cleared before those on which the section 455 tax has been paid. Clearing loans made in this period will save tax/create a repayment of 32.5% of the amount repaid.
4.   Loans made before 6 April 2016. This will generate a repayment of 25% of the amount repaid.

Choose Which Loans To Repay

Clark is the director of his personal company C Ltd. The company prepares it accounts to 30 June each year.

Clark has taken loans from the company as follows:

- A loan of £20,000 on 10 May 2022.
- A loan of £40,000 on 31 March 2020.
- A loan of £10,000 on 1 June 2015.

Section 455 tax of £13,000 (£40,000 @.5%) was paid on the loan of £40,000 on 1 April 2021 and section 455 tax of £2,500 (£10,000 @ 25%) was paid on the loan of £10,000 on 1 April 2016.

If the loan of £20,000 remains unpaid on 1 April 2023, C Ltd will need to pay section 455 tax of £6,750 (£20,000 @ 33.75%).

Clark is planning to sell some shares in December 2022 to raise £30,000 to start clearing the loans.

It makes sense to clear the loan of £20,000 made in May 2022 first. If this is done before 1 April 2023, C Ltd will not need to pay section 455 tax of £6,750.

The remaining £10,000 should be used to clear £10,000 of the loan made in March 2020. If the repayment is made in December 2022 (which falls in the year to 30 June 2023), C Ltd will be entitled to a repayment of £3,250 (£10,000 @ 32.5%) on 1 April 2024.

If he had cleared the earliest loan first he would have received a payment of £2,500. Using the balance to clear £20,000 of the

March 2020 loan would have generated a further repayment of £6,500.

The money is better utilised clearing the later loans which attract a higher rate of section 455 tax.

34. Employ Your Family

If a member of your family has no other income, you could employ them in your family business and save a significant amount of tax for the family as a whole.

Care must be taken to ensure that the arrangement is commercial, and the level of pay is commensurate with the duties performed, to avoid an attack from HMRC.

The National Minimum Wage rules also need to be considered, although the National Minimum Wage legislation does not apply to directors unless they have a contract of employment.

Employ Your Family

John's wife Kelly has no income but spends a considerable amount of time answering the telephone in John's home office and dealing with emails and correspondence. She also has the task of keeping track of the accounts, for which she is not paid.

By paying her a salary, he can reduce his own exposure to higher rate tax and utilise her personal allowance and, depending on the level of salary, her basic rate band, and reward her for the efforts she puts in on behalf of the business.

For example, assuming that Kelly has no other income, paying a salary equal to her personal allowance of £12,570 and reducing the salary paid to John (a higher rate taxpayer) by the same amount will save tax of £5,028 (£12,570 @ 40%). This simple strategy can save several thousand pounds in tax along the way.

Chapter 4:
Employers And Employees

35. Quarterly PAYE Payments

For employers, an important cash flow advantage can be obtained by making PAYE payments quarterly rather than monthly.

This is a choice available to employers whose payments to HMRC do not exceed £1,500 per month on average.

Quarterly PAYE Payments

Richard has one full-time employee, and his total PAYE deductions per month average less than £1,500.

He chooses to pay by quarterly instalments and hence has the use of up to £4,500 for a couple of months.

This can be a very useful payment strategy when money may be tight. It also reduces administration, as Richard only needs to make payments to HMRC four times a year rather than 12.

However, it should be noted that this does not affect the amount payable to HMRC, just the timing of the payments.

36. Pay PAYE On Time To Avoid Penalties

Penalties are charged if PAYE is paid late on more than one occasion in the tax year.

The penalty charged for late payment is a percentage of the PAYE paid late.

The penalty rate is linked to the number of occasions on which payment was made late in the tax year, ranging from 1% if payment is made late on two, three or four occasions in the year to 4% if payment is made late on 11 or 12 occasions. The penalty is charged in-year on a quarterly basis.

An additional penalty of 5% is charged if payment is outstanding after six months. If payment remains due after 12 months, a further 5% penalty is levied.

A PAYE month runs to the 5th of each month. Where payment is made electronically, cleared funds must reach HMRC's bank account by the 22nd of the month. Payments of PAYE and NIC must reach HMRC by the 19th of the month if paid by cheque. But see Tip 37 below where the normal payment date falls on a weekend or bank holiday.

37. Allow For Bank Holidays When Making PAYE Payments

As highlighted in Tip 36, PAYE should be paid on time each month to avoid late payment penalties.

However, to avoid getting caught out by bank holidays and weekends, ensure that payment is made early when the normal payment day falls on a bank holiday or a weekend. When this happens, the payment (or in the case of electronic payments, cleared funds) must reach HMRC by the last working day before the bank holiday or weekend on which the normal payment day falls.

In the 2022/23 tax year, particular care should be taken when paying by cheque in June 2022, November 2022, February 2023 and March 2023 when the 19th of the month falls at the weekend. Where payment is made electronically, care should be taken in May 2022, October 2022, and January 2023, when the 22nd of the month falls on the weekend. Payments should be sent early to ensure the deadline is met.

Allow For Bank Holidays When Making PAYE Payments

Jake pays his PAYE by cheque each month, posting the cheque on the 16th of the month to allow sufficient time for posting. His payment for PAYE month 7 (month to 5 November 2022) must reach HMRC by 19 November 2022.

However, as this falls on a Saturday, in reality, it must reach HMRC the previous Friday (18 November 2022).

Jake must, therefore, post his cheque by 15 November rather than 16 November to allow the same window to ensure it reaches HMRC on time.

If the cheque arrived on Saturday 19 November 2022, it would be treated by HMRC as having been received on Monday 21 November 2022 and the payment would be regarded as late. If Jake then paid late on one more occasion during 2022/23, he would suffer a late payment penalty.

This can be avoided by posting the cheque a few days early when the normal payment date falls on a weekend (or by making the payment electronically to take advantage of the later deadline).

38. Submit RTI Returns On Time

Under real-time information (RTI), employers must report details of pay and deductions to HMRC by means of a full payment submission (FPS) 'on or before' the date on which payment is made to the employee. Where no payments are made to employees in the tax month, employers must notify HMRC of this by filing an employer payment summary (EPS). This means that employers submit an FPS to HMRC on or before each payday in the month.

Penalties are charged for late returns. No penalty is charged for the first month that returns are made late. Thereafter a penalty is levied for each month in which one or more returns is made late. The penalty ranges from £100 to £400 depending on the number of employees in the PAYE scheme. An additional penalty of 5% is charged if the return is three months late. The penalty will be charged in-year on a quarterly basis.

While HMRC does allow a three-day period of grace before a penalty is charged, this is a concession, not a right and should be regarded as an occasional 'get out of jail free' card rather than an extension of the deadline. Employers who regularly file within this three-day window may be contacted by HMRC or considered for a penalty.

39. Reduce Your Employer's NIC Bill By £4,000

Employers are able to claim an NIC allowance of up to £4,000 for 2022/23 to set against their employer's NIC bill. The allowance is given as a reduction in the employer's NIC paid to HMRC, rather than by way of cashback. The allowance is set at £4,000 for 2022/23, but is capped at the amount of the secondary Class 1 National Insurance liability where this is lower. However, it should be noted that the employment allowance is not available to one-man companies where the sole employee is also a director.

There are also a small number of organisations that are not eligible, including employers of persons employed for personal, household or domestic work and those carrying out services of a public nature, such as GPs. Larger companies whose employer's Class 1 National Insurance liability was £100,000 or more in the previous tax year cannot now claim the employment allowance. The allowance is claimed through the RTI process by means of the employer payment summary. It does not have to be claimed at the start of the year; indeed it can be claimed at any point in the year.

Reduce Your Employer's NIC Bill By £4,000

XYZ Ltd has a monthly employer's NIC liability of £900. The company has five members of staff. For 2022/23, the company is eligible to claim the NIC employment allowance of £4,000. As a result, the employer's NIC liability is reduced to nil for months one, two, three and four, and to £500 for month five (the remaining £400 of the employment allowance being set against the employer's NIC bill of £900 for the month). From month six onwards, the full employer's NIC liability must be paid over to

HMRC. The employment allowance is claimed each month until it is fully utilised via the employment payment summary.

By claiming the employment allowance, XYZ Ltd reduces its annual employer's NIC bill by £4,000.

40. Use Basic PAYE Tools

To meet their obligations under real-time information (RTI), employers must use RTI-compliant payroll software. There are numerous software solutions available.

However, employers with nine or fewer employees can use HMRC's free Basic PAYE Tools software package to meet their obligations under RTI without having to spend money on a commercial software package.

Basic PAYE Tools can be downloaded from the GOV.UK website (see www.gov.uk/basic-paye-tools).

41. Take Advantage Of The Exemption For Paid And Reimbursed Expenses

The statutory exemption for qualifying paid and reimbursed expenses means that employers do not need to report expenses to HMRC if the expense would be deductible if paid by the employee him or herself. Employee expenses are deductible if they are incurred wholly, exclusively, and necessarily for the purposes of the employment. Examples of expenses that would be deductible if met by the employee include travel expenses for business trips, professional fees, and subscriptions. Thus, under the terms of the exemption, if the employer pays or reimburses these expenses, there is nothing to report to HMRC and no tax to pay by the employee.

Note: the benefit of the exemption is lost if the payment or reimbursement is made via an optional remuneration arrangement such as a salary sacrifice scheme. Where this is the case, the alternative valuation rules apply.

Take Advantage Of The Exemption For Paid And Reimbursed Expenses

GHI Ltd has a number of employees who are regularly required to travel for business, often by train. The employees pay for the travel initially and reclaim the expenses from the company by completing an expenses claim form.

The travel expenses would be deductible if met by the employees themselves. Consequently, the exemption for paid and reimbursed expenses applies and the amounts reimbursed do not need to be reported to HMRC and there is no tax for the employee to pay.

Similarly, the employees are spared the hassle of claiming the tax deduction – the amounts are simply ignored by the tax system.

42. Claim A Deduction For Mileage Payments

Under the Approved Mileage Allowance Payments (AMAP) Scheme, employers can pay employees tax-free mileage rates when they use their own car for business. Provided that the amounts paid do not exceed the rates set by HMRC, no tax liability arises and there is nothing to report on the P11D or to payroll where the employer has elected to tax benefits through the payroll.

However, many employees are unaware that if their employer pays them at a rate that is less than the approved rate, they can claim a tax deduction for the shortfall. The approved mileage rates for 2022/23 for cars and vans are 45p per mile for the first 10,000 business miles in the tax year and 25p per mile thereafter.

Claim A Deduction For Mileage Payments

Nigel uses his own car for work and in 2022/23 undertakes 9,000 business miles. His employer pays a mileage allowance of 30p per mile. Thus, Nigel receives mileage allowances of £2,700 during the year.

However, at the approved rate of 45p per mile for the first 10,000 business miles, Nigel's employer could pay him a tax-free allowance of £4,050 (9,000 miles at 45p per mile). This is known as 'the approved amount'.

Nigel can claim a tax deduction of £1,350 for the shortfall between the approved amount (£4,050) and the amount he is actually paid (£2,700). If Nigel is a higher rate taxpayer paying tax at 40%, this will save him tax of £540.

43. Company Cars – Make Green Choices

The appropriate percentage for the car benefit charge and the fuel scale charge is linked to the level of carbon dioxide emissions from the car, and the higher the CO_2 emissions, the higher the appropriate percentage (until the maximum charge of 37% is reached). This means that you will pay more tax on a car with high CO_2 emissions than on one with the same list price, but lower CO_2 emissions. Therefore, by choosing a lower emission company car, you can save considerable amounts in tax.

Zero emission cars (regardless of when they are first registered) have an appropriate percentage of 2% for 2022/23, making an electric car a very tax-efficient benefit.

The electric range of a hybrid car is also taken into account in determining the appropriate percentage of cars whose emissions fall within the 1–50g/km. Cars with the greatest electric range (also referred to as 'zero emission mileage') have the lowest appropriate percentage. The appropriate percentage is 2% if the car's electric range is more than 130 miles. By contrast, where the electric range is less than 30 miles, the charge is 14%. Choosing a hybrid with a good electric range can save large amounts of tax.

At the other end of the scale, for 2022/23, the maximum charge of 37% applies to cars with CO_2 emissions of 160g/km and above.

A supplement applies to diesel cars that do not meet the Real Driving Emissions 2 (RDE2) standard. The supplement is set at 4% and applies to diesel cars registered on or after 1 January 1998 that either do not have a registered Nitrogen Oxide (NOx) emissions value or which have NOx emissions that exceed the RDE2 standard. The addition of the diesel supplement cannot take the appropriate percentage above the maximum charge of 37%.

To minimise the benefit-in-kind charge (and the associated employer's National Insurance) choose a car with low or zero emissions – the lower the emissions, the lower the tax charge.

Where fuel is provided for private mileage, choosing a lower emission car will also reduce the fuel benefit tax charge.

Company Cars – Make Green Choices

Bill is a higher rate taxpayer and pays tax at 40%. He works for ABC Ltd.

He has a company car costing £30,000 with CO2 emissions of 60g/km. The appropriate percentage for 2022/23 is 17% and the amount charged to tax is £5,100. As Bill is a higher rate taxpayer, he will pay tax on the benefit of £2,040. His employer will pay Class 1A National Insurance of £767.55 (£5,100 @ 15.05%).

Had Bill chosen a car with the same list price but with CO2 emissions of 180g/km, the maximum charge of 37% would apply and he would be taxed on a benefit with a value of £11,100, giving rise to a tax charge at 40% of £4,440. His employer would pay Class 1A National Insurance of £1,670.55 (£11,100 @ 15.05%).

By choosing a lower emission model, Bill saves tax of £2,400 and his employer pays £903 less Class 1A National Insurance.

44. Company Cars – Electric Cars And Hybrid Cars

For 2022/23, the appropriate percentage for a zero emission car is 2%. This makes an electric car a tax-efficient benefit. For example, a higher rate taxpayer will only pay tax of £320 on an electric company car with a list price of £40,000 that is available for his or her private use throughout the 2022/23 tax year. The taxable amount of the benefit is £800 (£40,000 @ 2%).

The appropriate percentage for cars that fall in the 1 to 50g/km band depends on the electric range of the car – the greater the electric range, the lower the appropriate percentage.

A car with an electric range of 130 miles and CO_2 emissions of 1–50g/km has an appropriate percentage of 2%, whereas one with the same CO_2 emissions but an electric range of less than 30 miles has an appropriate percentage of 14%.

The appropriate percentages for 2022/23 for cars with CO_2 emissions of 1–50g/km is shown in the following table.

CO2 Emissions	Electric Range	Appropriate Percentage
1–50g/km	130 miles or more	2%
	70–129 miles	5%

	40–69 miles	8%
	30–39 miles	12%
	Less than 30 miles	14%

Cars with CO2 emissions of 51-54g/km have an appropriate percentage of 15%. Thereafter, the appropriate percentage increases, in each case, by one percentage point for every 5g/km increase in CO2 emissions until the maximum charge of 37% applies.

Employers should consider providing electric cars or hybrid cars with the greatest possible electric range.

Not only will choosing electric or very low emissions cars save the employee tax, the employer will also pay less Class 1A National Insurance. As Class 1A National Insurance is charged at 15.05% for 2022/23, this is a worthwhile saving.

A further advantage of electric cars is that there is no 'fuel' benefit charge if the employer meets the cost of electricity for private motoring – HMRC do not regard electricity as a fuel for these purposes.

Company Cars – Electric Cars And Hybrid Cars

Charlie is environmentally conscious. He needs a company car for work and chooses an electric car. The car has a list price of £25,000.

For 2022/23, the appropriate percentage for a zero emissions car is only 2%. The value of the benefit for tax purposes is therefore £500, and as a higher rate taxpayer Charlie only pays tax of £200 for the benefit of the car. His employer's Class 1A National Insurance is only £75.25 (£500 @ 15.05%).

Choosing an electric car is therefore a very tax-efficient benefit.

45. Cut The Fuel Benefit Charge

The fuel benefit charge can be very expensive as the fuel multiplier by reference to which the charge is worked out is high – set at £25,300 for 2022/23. Consequently, it may be the case that you pay more tax on the fuel than on the company car. This will be the case where the list price of the car is less than the fuel multiplier. You may also find that you pay more in tax for the benefit of private fuel than you actually spend on fuel for private mileage.

There are various ways to reduce the tax payable in respect of fuel:

- Changing to a company car with a lower emissions rating will reduce the appropriate percentage and consequently the fuel benefit charge.

- Reimbursing the company for every drop of fuel used privately will reduce the fuel scale charge to nil. Eliminating the benefit eliminates the associated tax charge. To make this work, the employee needs to be required to reimburse the full cost of all private fuel and must actually do so by 6 July following the end of the tax year. If your private mileage is low, this can be a valuable tax saving for both you and the company. Reimbursement can be made using actual costs or the HMRC advisory fuel rates.

- Changing to an electric company car will allow the employer to meet the cost of private motoring without the employee suffering the fuel scale charge. This is because HMRC does not regard electricity as 'fuel' for the purposes of the fuel scale charge. Consequently, the employer can meet the cost of electricity for private journeys in a company car without triggering the fuel benefit charge.

Cut The Fuel Benefit Charge

Alberto has a company car with an appropriate percentage of 25% in 2022/23. His employer pays for all fuel.

If Alberto does not reimburse the cost of private fuel, he will suffer a fuel benefit charge of £6,325 for 2022/23 (£25,300 @ 25%). As a higher rate taxpayer, this will cost him £2,530 in tax. Alberto estimates that he spends £100 a month on fuel – an annual fuel spend of £1,200. If Alberto paid for fuel himself, this would be equivalent to gross pay of £2,114 after allowing for tax of 40% and employee's National Insurance of 3.25%).

As the tax on the fuel benefit is more than the amount of his pre-tax pay that he spends on fuel, the benefit of free fuel is not worthwhile. Reimbursing the cost of all fuel for private motoring will prevent the fuel charge from applying, which will save Alberto money.

Where the fuel benefit is eliminated, the company saves Class 1A NIC at 15.05% on the value of the benefit.

46. Company Car Or Car Allowance?

Company cars are highly taxed and the opportunity to swap your company car for a car allowance and provide your own car from the allowance may seem an attractive option.

However, there is no substitute for doing the maths and the employee should compare the cost of the different options. There is no point saving the tax if the employee ends up out of pocket. In comparing the options, all costs of running the car – servicing, insurance, etc. – should be taken into account.

If a cash alternative is offered instead of a car, and the car is chosen, where the car has CO_2 emissions of more than 75g/km, the alternative valuation rules apply and the car will be taxed by reference to the cash alternative offered if this is more than the cash equivalent of the car calculated under the normal rules. This is something to be aware of when offering a cash alternative.

Company Car Or Car Allowance?

Bill is an employee. He has a company car with a cash equivalent value of £9,500. He pays tax at 40%. The tax cost of having a company car is £3,800 (£9,500 @ 40%). The CO_2 emissions of the car are more than 75g/km.

He travels 10,000 miles per annum on business, and the company offers him a car allowance of £6,000 per annum instead of his company car. He will pay tax of £2,400 on the allowance and National Insurance of £195. He will need to fund a car and the cost of funding the car should be taken into account in the calculations.

When he uses the car for business, Bill is able to claim a tax-free mileage allowance. The allowance is paid at the tax-free rate of 45p per mile for the first 10,000 miles, a total tax-free allowance of £4,500 (10,000 miles at 45p per mile).

By taking the allowance rather than the car, Bill will be better off in cash terms, as he will save the tax on the company car and will receive the car allowance and mileage allowance. If this exceeds the cost of providing and running his own car, he is better off by taking the allowance than the company car.

If he had chosen the car, the car would have been taxed by reference to the cash equivalent value, as this is higher than the cash allowance.

47. Putting Your Mobile Phone Through The Company

An employee can be provided with the use a mobile phone tax-free. This can amount to a valuable tax-free benefit.

For the exemption to apply, the contract for the provision of the phone must be between the mobile phone provider and the company. The exemption does not apply if the contract is between the employee and the phone company and the company pays the bill on the employee's behalf – in this case, the company is meeting a personal liability rather than providing the employee with a phone.

This distinction is important.

HMRC accepts that smartphones fall within the scope of the exemption.

The exemption is limited to one phone per employee.

However, to ensure that the tax exemption is not lost, the phone must not be made available via a salary sacrifice or other optional remuneration arrangement. Where provision is made via an optional remuneration arrangement, the alternative valuation rules bite and the employee will be taxed by reference to the salary given up in exchange for the phone.

Putting Your Mobile Phone Through The Company

James is the director of his personal company J Ltd. The company provides him with a mobile phone. The contract is between J Ltd and the mobile phone company and costs J Ltd £35 per month (£420 a year). This is a tax-free benefit in James' hands. The cost is deductible in computing the profits of the company for corporation tax purposes.

There is no benefit-in-kind charge on the phone.

If James had met the cost of the phone himself, he would have spent £420 out of his after-tax (and NIC) income. If he was a higher rate taxpayer, this would use up £740 of his gross pay.

48. Tax-Free Benefits Using Salary Sacrifice Arrangements

Although the introduction of the alternative valuation rules has seriously curtailed the benefits of using a salary sacrifice arrangement, there are still limited circumstances when a salary sacrifice arrangement can still be worthwhile. The alternative valuation rules do not apply to the following benefits, and thus the associated tax exemptions remain available where provision is made via a salary sacrifice arrangement:

- employer-provided pension savings;
- employer-provided pension advice;
- childcare vouchers;
- employer-supported childcare;
- workplace nurseries;
- employer-provided cycles and cyclists' safety equipment (including 'cycle to work' schemes).

Providing any benefit from the above list under a salary sacrifice arrangement will enable the employee to save the tax that would have been payable on the cash salary, and for the employee and the employer to save the Class 1 National Insurance that would have been paid had the employee continued to receive the 'sacrificed' salary .In addition to the benefits listed above, the alternative valuation rules do not apply to low emission cars with CO_2 emissions of 75g/km or less (which when provided are taxed according to the company car tax rules rather than in relation to any salary foregone or cash alternative offered).It should be noted the tax exemption for employer-provided childcare vouchers and employer-supported childcare is only available to employees who had joined their employer's scheme by 4 October 2018. However, employees within a scheme at that date can remain in it and benefit from the associated exemptions while their employer continues to operate the scheme. However, the employee should consider whether they would be better using the government's tax-free top-up scheme instead of their employer's scheme – it is not possible to benefit from both.

A salary sacrifice scheme allows the employer to offer employees the opportunity to benefit from the tax exemptions available for the benefits listed above, without having to meet the cost of providing those benefits – the cost is passed on to the employee and funded from the salary that they give up in exchange for the benefit.

A salary sacrifice arrangement can also generate National Insurance savings for the employee where the benefit provided is either not exempt from tax or the exemption is lost as a result of the alternative valuation rules coming into play. The employee's National Insurance saving results from replacing cash salary (which is liable to employee and employer Class 1 contributions) with a non-cash benefit which is liable to employer-only Class 1A contributions, saving employee contributions in the process. However, when taking into account the administrative costs of administering the salary sacrifice arrangement, this may only be worthwhile if the National Insurance savings are significant.

Tax-Free Benefits Using Salary Sacrifice Arrangements

Lucy has been in her employer's childcare voucher scheme since 2016 and via a salary sacrifice scheme, she has opted to swap salary of £55 per week for childcare vouchers. As a basic rate taxpayer, this saves her £11 per week in tax and £7.28 per week in employee's National Insurance. Her employer also saves employer's National Insurance of £8.27 a week – combined savings of over £1,300 a year. A win-win situation.

49. Working Abroad – Tax-Free Trips For Your Family

If you are sent to work abroad for a continuous period of at least 60 days, then your employer can pay for two trips abroad per tax year for your spouse or civil partner and children without any charge to tax on the costs arising on you.

Care should be taken to space the trips out so that only two per tax year are paid for to avoid a benefit-in-kind charge arising.

If necessary, delay or bring forward a trip to ensure good use of this concession.

Working Abroad – Tax-Free Trips For Your Family

In January 2023, Daniel is sent by his employer to work in Dubai for 12 months.

His employer can pay for two trips each tax year for Daniel's wife and children.

Because his work started in January 2023, he could get four trips paid for in 2023 without suffering a taxable benefit.

This is achieved by taking two trips in the 2022/23 tax year (i.e. before 6 April 2023) and two in the 2023/24 tax year (i.e. after 5 April 2023).

50. Claiming Tax Relief For Expenses

If you incur expenses in doing your job, you may be able to claim tax relief for those expenses. Relief is available for expenses which are wholly, necessarily and exclusively incurred in performing the duties of your employment.

If you need to complete a self-assessment tax return, you can claim tax relief for any deductible employment expenses on the employment pages of the return.

If you do not fill in a tax return, there are various ways in which you can claim tax relief for employment expenses. A claim can be made online (see https://www.gov.uk/guidance/claim-income-tax-relief-for-your-employment-expenses-p87). A claim can also be made by post. A form is available on the Gov.uk website which can be completed on screen and printed off (see www.gov.uk/guidance/claim-income-tax-relief-for-your-employment-expenses-p87#claim-by-post). Postal claims can only be made on form P87, not by letter.

Alternatively, where expenses have already been claimed for a previous year and the total expenses are either less than £1,000 (or £2,500 where they relate to professional fees and subscriptions), the claim can be made by phone.

Claiming Tax Relief For Expenses

Chris is an employee. Each year he pays professional fees and subscriptions of £700 which are relevant to his job.

The subscriptions are payable to a body on HMRC's approved list. Chris does not receive any other benefit and does not need to submit a tax return.

He can claim relief for the expenses by phone.

The relief is worth £140 to a basic rate taxpayer and £280 to a 40% taxpayer. Had Chris not claimed the relief, he would have missed out.

Chapter 5:
Self-Employed

51. No Class 2 Or Class 4 NICs For Low Earners

52. Paying Class 2 NICs Voluntarily

53. Choosing A 31 March Accounting Date For A New Business

54. Consider Changing Your Accounting Date To 31 March

55. Choosing A Cessation Date

56. Use The Cash Basis To Calculate Taxable Income And Save Work

57. Claim Simplified Expenses

58. Self-Employed? Consider If Incorporation Is Worthwhile?

51. No Class 2 Or Class 4 NICs For Low Earners

If your earnings from your self-employment are less than the small profits threshold, set at £6,725 for 2022/23, you do not have to pay any Class 2 NIC for that year. The liability to Class 2 does not arise until profits from self-employment reach the small profits threshold, although the self-employed whose profits are below this level can choose to pay Class 2 voluntarily if they so wish (see Tip 52).

Where profits are below the lower profits limit for Class 4 (set at £11,908 for 2022/23), there are no Class 4 contributions to pay either.

Note: The National Insurance Contributions (Increase of Thresholds) Act 2022 contains provision for regulations to be made to increase the starting point for Class 2 contributions so as to align it with the starting threshold for Class 4 National Insurance contributions (£11,908). This will mean that where profits were below the lower profits limit, an self-employed earner will pay no National Insurance contributions. However, so that self-employed earners with low profits do not lose entitlement to the state pension, the Act also makes provision for regulations to be made with retrospective effect no earlier than 6 April 2022 to treat self-employed earners with profits below the threshold as having paid Class 2 contributions. At the time of writing, the regulations had not been made.

52. Paying Class 2 NICs Voluntarily

For 2022/23, you are not required to pay Class 2 NICs if your earnings from self-employment are less than the small profits threshold of £6,725. However, if you have no other earnings and are not entitled to NIC credits, you may wish to pay Class 2 contributions voluntarily to preserve entitlement to the state pension, as this is much cheaper than paying Class 3 (voluntary) contributions, which for 2022/23 are £15.85 a week compared to £3.15 per week for Class 2 contributions. Paying Class 2 contributions voluntarily rather than Class 3 will save £12.70 a week in 2022/23, a yearly saving of £660.

However, before opting to pay Class 2 contributions, check whether you already have 35 qualifying years. You need 35 qualifying years to receive a full state pension, and once you have enough, there is no benefit in paying voluntary contributions as this will not increase the pension that you receive. Note: The National Insurance Contributions (Increase of Thresholds) Act 2022 contains provision for regulations to be made to increase the starting point for Class 2 contributions so as to align it with the starting threshold for Class 4 National Insurance contributions (£11,908). This will mean that where profits were below the lower profits limit, an self-employed earner will pay no National Insurance contributions. However, so that self-employed earners with low profits do not lose entitlement to the state pension, the Act also makes provision for regulations to be made with retrospective effect no earlier than 6 April 2022 to treat self-employed earners with profits below the threshold as having paid Class 2 contributions. This will remove the need to pay Class 2 (or Class 3) contributions voluntarily. At the time of writing, the regulations had not been made.

Paying Class 2 NICs Voluntarily

Louisa is a self-employed hairdresser. She prepares her accounts to 30 April each year. As a result of the Covid-19 pandemic, she lost a lot of business, and her profits for the year to 30 April 2022 were £6,000.

As her earnings are below the small profits threshold of £6,725 for 2022/23, she is not liable to pay Class 2 National Insurance contributions. However, she chooses to pay them voluntarily, as at £3.15 a week this is a cheap way to build up her entitlement to the state pension.

53. Choosing A 31 March Accounting Date For A New Business

For 2022/23, subject to opening and closing year rules, the profits that are taxed for a tax year are those of the accounting period ending in that tax year.

The rules on taxing profits from self-employment are changing from 2024/25. From 2024/25, the profits that will be taxed for a tax year are those for that tax year (i.e. from 6 April to the following 5 April). Where accounts are prepared to a date other than 31 March/5 April, it will be necessary to apportion profits from two accounting periods to arrive at the profits for the tax year.

For existing businesses without a 31 March/5 April year end, 2023/24 is a transition year to move them to the tax year basis.

If you are starting a business in 2022/23, it will be easier to choose a 31 March year end as this will make life more straightforward once profits are taxed on a tax year basis.

Choose A 31 March Accounting Date For A New Business

William starts self-employment on 1 July 2022.

To make life easier going forward, he chooses an accounting date of 31 March.

He will be taxed on the profits for the period from 1 July 2022 to 31 March 2023. These are his profits from the date of commencement to the first accounting date. As the accounting date of 31 March falls in the period 31 March to 4 April, the accounting date is used rather than the end of the tax year.

For 2023/24, he is taxed on the profits to 31 March 2024.

As his accounting date corresponds with the tax year, he will be taxed on the profits of the year to 31 March 2025 for 2024/25, the profits of the year to 31 March 2026 for 2025/26 and so on.

54. Consider Changing Your Accounting Date To 31 March

From 2024/25 profits will be taxed on a tax year basis. This means that if you do not prepare your accounts to 31 March (or a date between 1 and 5 April), you will need to apportion the profits from two accounting periods to arrive at the profit for the tax year. For example, if you prepare accounts to 30 June each year, for 2024/25 you will be taxed on $3/12^{th}$ of your profits for the year to 30 June 2024 and $9/12^{th}$ of your profits for the year to 30 June 2025. This will involve additional work and mean that you need two sets of accounts to arrive at the taxable profits for the tax year.

If you prepare accounts to a date other than 31 March (or between 1 and 5 April), 2023/24 will be a transitional year. You will be taxed on:

1.   The profits for the accounting period ending in 2023/23 (i.e. those taxable under the current year basis). This is the standard component,
2.   The profits from the end of that accounting period to 5 April 2024 This is the transition component.

You will be able to deduct any overlap relief from profits taxed twice on commencement or on a change of accounting date. The rules will mean that you will be taxed on more than 12 months' profits in 2023/24 However, to ease the cash flow burden of this, you can opt to spread the transition profits over five years starting with 2023/24.

To avoid the complications with apportioning profits going forward, you may wish to move to an accounting date of 31 March. If you wish to do this, you will have to decide when to make the change. This could be done in 2022/23 or in the transition year of 2023/24.

If you change your accounting date in 2022/23, you will need to move to an accounting date of 31 March 2023. If the change results in a period of

18 months or less, you can prepare a single set of accounts. If you have overlap profits, you will be able to deduct these subject to the restrictions where the period of overlap profits is longer than the amount by which the length of the accounting period exceeds 12 months. If the interval for which accounts need to be prepared is more than 18 months, you will need to prepare two sets of accounts, one for 12 months and one for the balance.

If you opt to change your accounting date in the transitional year, moving to an accounting date of 31 March 2024, you will be able to access spreading relief and also obtain relief for overlap profits in that year.

Do the sums to see what works best for you.

Consider Changing Your Accounting Date To 31 March

Freddie has been in business as a sole trader for many years preparing accounts to 31 December each year.

He started his business on 1 January 2000, and has overlap profits of £10,000 relating to the period from 1 January 2000 to 5 April 2000.

He wants to move to a tax year basis, changing his accounting date to 31 March.

If he changes his accounting date in 2022/23, he will be taxed on profits for the 15 months from 1 January 2022 to 31 March 2023, less the overlap profits. This will mean he will pay tax on more than 12 months' profits for 2022/23.

However, if he waits until the transitional year of 2023/24, he will be able to claim spreading relief for the profits from 1 January 2024 to 31 March 2024, which will ease the cash flow burden of the move. Relief will also be given for overlap profits.

55. Choosing A Cessation Date

If your self-employment comes to an end, either naturally or through the decision to incorporate, if you plan to cease trading in 2022/23 it pays to be careful when choosing the date on which you cease trading, as this can have a major bearing on the amount of tax payable in the final year.

Choosing A Cessation Date

William started trading on 1 July 2010. He chose an accounting date of 30 April to maximise the window before tax on the profits of the period had to be paid.

Under the current year basis, he was taxed twice on the profits from 1 July 2010 to 5 April 2011. These are his overlap profits.

The final basis period begins immediately after the end of the basis period for the previous tax year and ends on the date of cessation.

The basis period for 2021/22 is the year to 30 April 2021.

If William chooses to cease self-employment on 31 March 2023, he will be taxed on 23 months' profit in one year with very little in the way of overlap relief.

If, however, he ceases on 1 May 2022 in the tax year, he will be taxed on the final 12 months of profit only.

This will spread the bill more evenly.

This shows that timing the cessation date correctly can save considerable tax.

56. Use The Cash Basis To Calculate Taxable Income And Save Work

For traders, taxable profits are normally calculated in accordance with Generally Accepted Accounting Practice. This means that profits are determined on the accruals basis by reference to the amount earned in the year, rather than by reference to cash received and paid out.

However, eligible small businesses can elect to use the simpler cash basis to work out taxable profits. Under the cash basis, income is taken into account when received and expenses are recognised when paid. There is no need to match earnings to the period to which they relate, or take account of debtors or creditors, or prepayments or accruals.

An election applies for the tax year for which it is made and for subsequent tax years. The cash basis option is only available to the self-employed and to individuals in partnership whose receipts are not more than £150,000. Once in the cash basis, a trader can remain in it as long as profits do not exceed £300,000. The thresholds are doubled where the claimant receives universal credit.

By contrast, the cash basis is the default basis for unincorporated property businesses that meet the cash eligibility criteria. This means that it will apply to an unincorporated property business automatically if the eligibility criteria are met – no election is required. However, the property business can opt out and instead use the accruals basis if this is preferred.

One advantage of the cash basis is that it provides automatic relief for bad debts as income is not recognised until it is received.

Under the cash basis, there are fewer options for relieving losses and interest relief is limited to £500 per year. Different rules also apply in relation to capital expenditure.

Before opting for the cash basis, check that it is beneficial for your business.

Use The Cash Basis To Calculate Taxable Income And Save Work

Martha is a self-employed gardener. In May 2022, she undertook some work for a commercial client, billing them £4,000. However, the client went into liquidation and was not able to pay Martha's bill.

As Martha prepares accounts on the cash basis, the bill was not taken into account in calculating her taxable profits as it would have only been recognised when paid. In this way, she receives automatic and immediate relief for the bad debt.

57. Claim Simplified Expenses

To save some of the work incurred in keeping details of expenses, individuals carrying on a trade as a self-employed sole trader or in partnership with other individuals can instead claim fixed rate deductions.

Fixed rate deductions are available in respect of vehicle deductions, business use of home, and in relation to business premises which are also used as a home.

For 2022/23, the appropriate mileage rate for cars and vans is 45p per mile for the first 10,000 business miles and 25p per mile thereafter. The appropriate mileage rate for motorcycles is 24p per mile. Simplified expenses cannot be used for cars in respect of which capital allowances have been claimed.

Where the home is used for business, a fixed monthly deduction, as shown in the following table, is allowed in respect of the household costs related to the use of the home for business. The amount of the deduction depends on the number of hours for which the home is used for the purposes of the business.

Number of hours worked at home in month	Monthly deduction
25 to 50	£10
51 to 100	£18
101 or more	£26

Where the business premises are also the home (for example, as would be the case for a bed and breakfast business where the proprietor lives on the premises), a fixed amount is disallowed each month in respect of personal use. The amount of the disallowance depends on the number of people living in the premises, as shown in the following table.

Number of people	Monthly disallowance
1	£350
2	£500
3 or more	£650

Businesses can choose to use simplified expenses to save work. Alternatively, they can keep records of actual expenditure and make the necessary apportionments between home and business use. Where records are kept, businesses have the option of claiming a deduction for either the actual expense or, where this gives a more favourable result, claiming the fixed rate deduction.

Claim Simplified Expenses

Lucy works from home running a small business making soft toys. She works 30 hours a week.

To save paperwork, she claims a fixed rate deduction of £26 per month (the rate applicable where hours worked at home in a month are 101 or more) for use of her home for business purposes.

58. Self-Employed? Consider If Incorporation Is Worthwhile

It can still be beneficial to incorporate and extract funds by taking a small salary and extracting further profits in the form of dividends (See Tips 24, 25 and 26).

Dividends do not attract National Insurance contributions, so by incorporating and extracting profits as dividends, you will save Class 2 and Class 4 National Insurance contributions. Dividends also benefit from a £2,000 tax-free dividend allowance.

A typical tax-efficient profit extraction strategy is to pay a small salary up to the higher of the secondary threshold and the primary threshold (or the personal allowance if the employment allowance is available) and to extract further profits as dividends. Once the dividend allowance has been used up, dividends, taxed as the top slice of income, are for 2022/23 taxed at 8.75% to the extent they fall in the basic rate band, 33.75% to the extent that they fall within the higher rate band and at 39.35% where they fall in the additional rate band.

It should be noted that dividends can only be paid from retained profits and for each class of share, shareholders must receive dividends in proportion to their shareholdings.

As personal circumstances differ, there is no substitute for crunching the numbers. Consideration should also be given as to whether the costs of incorporation outweigh the tax and National Insurance savings.

Looking ahead, it should be noted that the rate of corporation tax is set to increase for companies with taxable profits of more than the lower limit (set at £50,000, divided by the number of associated companies plus one where the company has at least one associate) from 1 April 2023. From that date a small profits rate of 19% will apply where taxable profits do not exceed the lower limit, with a main rate of 25% applying where taxable profits are more than the lower limit. However, the effective rate will be reduced by marginal relief where profits are between the lower limit and the upper limit (set at £250,000 and divided by the number of associated companies plus one where the company has at least one associated company). These limits are reduced proportionately where the accounting period is less than 12 months. If you are deciding whether it is worthwhile incorporating, the impact of the future rises in the corporation tax rate should be taken into account.

Self-Employed? Consider If Incorporation Is Worthwhile

Harry incorporates on 1 April 2022 and makes a profit of £50,000 in his first year.

Not only does he now have a choice as to whether to draw this income and pay personal taxes on it or leave it in the company and only incur corporation tax on his profits, he also saves tax and National Insurance by extracting profits as dividends, because dividends do not attract National Insurance contributions and dividends are taxed at lower rates of tax.

However, dividends can only be paid out of retained profits, which have already suffered corporation tax at 19%.

Chapter 6:
Losses

59. Maximising Trading Losses

The use of losses for tax purposes is a complicated topic and many factors come into play.

However, a basic planning tip is to ensure that you are aware of the time limits for making claims and the methods of relief available. Traditional wisdom is to obtain relief for losses at the highest possible rate and as early as possible; however, personal circumstances will dictate the optimal route.

A self-employed person making a trading loss basically has the option to relieve the loss:

- this year,

- last year, or

- to carry it forward against future profits.

For 2020/21 and 2021/22 losses, extended loss relief applying for a limited period meant that the loss could be carried back against trading profits of the same trade for the previous three years, setting the loss against profits of a later year before an earlier year. A claim could only be made in respect of a loss which has not been used against income of the current or previous year.

Where accounts are prepared under the accruals basis, the loss can be relieved sideways against other income for the year of the loss and the previous year. The claim may also be extended to capital gains. These options are unavailable under the cash basis – the loss can only be relieved against profits of the same trade.

The decision as to which way to go will be dependent on a number of factors including:

- future profit levels

- other income for the year

- the level of income for the previous year

- the tax rates in each of those years.

Where a trader opts to use the cash basis, losses cannot be relieved sideways or against capital gains. However, under the extended carry back rules, a loss for 2020/21 or 2021/22 could be set against trading profits of the same trade for the previous three years.

It should be noted that there is a cap on certain reliefs, including loss reliefs, which can be claimed against general income. The cap is set at £50,000 or 25% of income if higher (see Tip 63.)

Maximising Trading Losses

Raymond has been in business as a sole trader for many years and makes an allowable trading loss of £30,000 for the accounting period ending 30 June 2022 (which falls in the 2022/23 tax year). He prepares accounts using the accruals basis. His income is derived purely from his business. The previous year's profits were £70,000, and he anticipates a profit of £20,000 the following year. He can carry back the loss in full to set against the profits of the previous year, recovering some tax at 40% and the balance at 20%.

60. The Loss Relief Extension To Capital Gains

Many people are unaware that if a trading loss is claimed against other income, either for the current or previous year, then by election this can be extended to capital gains, resulting in a further refund of taxes. This option is only available where the sole trader prepares accounts using the accruals basis. It cannot be used by traders who prepare accounts under the cash basis.

This can be of considerable benefit depending on the circumstances.

The Loss Relief Extension To Capital Gains

Steve makes a loss in 2022/23 of £50,000. He prepares accounts using the accruals basis. In 2022/23 he also has income from other sources of £30,000 and chargeable gains (after deducting the annual exemption) of £20,000. His profit for 2023/24 is estimated to be £10,000. Clearly, it is advantageous in this situation to relieve the loss sideways against his other income and extend the claim to cover the capital gains. Tax relief is obtained at the earliest opportunity. His anticipated profit for 2023/24 will be sheltered by his personal allowance.

61. Special Relief For Early Year Losses

A business often makes losses in the early years of the trade. There is a special loss relief available to individuals which allows a loss made in the tax year in which the individual first carried on the trade or in any of the three succeeding years, to be relieved against total income of the preceding three tax years.

The loss is relieved against the income of an earlier year before a later year. This relief is only available where the trader prepares accounts using the accruals basis. A claim cannot be used by traders preparing their accounts using the cash basis.

Where a loss is anticipated in the early years, the trader may wish to prepare accounts using the accruals basis rather than the cash basis to take advantage of the wider loss relief options available. Carrying back the loss relieves the loss at the earliest opportunity and generates a tax repayment.

Note: relief for certain losses is capped each year at the greater of 25% of income and £50,000. The cap applies to various types of loss relief and to relief for qualifying interest. In some cases, the operation of the cap may limit the amount of early years' loss relief that can be obtained. Further, if the cash basis is used, it is not possible to relieve losses sideways or to carry them back.

Special Relief For Early Year Losses

Joshua was previously employed on a salary of £80,000 per annum and makes a loss in his first year of trading of £20,000. He prepares his accounts using the accruals basis. He anticipates making a profit the following year of £10,000. Joshua can elect to carry this loss back three years and hence obtain tax relief on this loss both earlier and at a higher rate than would otherwise be achieved.

Using the accruals basis rather than the cash basis allows Joshua to access this valuable relief.

62. Relief For Losses On Cessation

A person may decide to stop trading if they are making losses. Although the loss can be relieved in the usual ways (as appropriate), an additional relief is available for the loss made on the cessation of the business (known as a terminal loss).

A claim for terminal loss relief can be made if the person permanently ceases to carry on a trade and makes a terminal loss. The terminal loss is the loss made in the period beginning at the start of the final tax year and ending with the date of cessation plus any loss in the last 12 months that falls into the previous tax year. The terminal loss may be relieved against the profits of the trade for the final tax year and the previous three tax years. Relief is given against a later year before an earlier year.

Alternatively, the loss can be set against total income (and extended to capital gains) of the year of the loss and/or the preceding year.

Relief For Losses On Cessation

Will has been in business as a sole trader for a number of years. He prepares accounts to 31 March each year. As a result of the impact of the Covid-19 pandemic, a key customer goes out of business meaning William's business is no longer viable. He ceases to trade on 30 June 2022.

He makes a profit of £10,000 for the year to 31 March 2022 and a loss of £16,000 for the period from 1 April 2022 to 30 June 2022. He has overlap profits of £5,000 to relieve, which are deducted in the final period.

His terminal loss for 2022/23 is £21,000 (loss in three months to 30 June 2022 of £16,000 plus overlap profits available for relief of £5,000).

He made profits of £9,000 for the year to 31 March 2021 (taxed in 2020/21) and £25,000 for the year to 31 March 2020 (taxed in 2019/20).

He claims terminal loss relief.

The loss is set first against the profit made in 2021/22 (£10,000) with £9,000 being set against the profits of 2020/21 and the remaining £2,000 carried back and set against the profits of 2019/20.

63. Losses And Capital Allowances

Capital allowances are treated as part of a trading loss for loss relief purposes, and so care should be taken to determine whether it is beneficial to claim capital allowances or not. Not claiming capital allowances (or claiming a writing down allowance instead of the annual investment allowance) to reduce the amount of the loss may actually leave you better off.

This is because personal allowances are ignored in loss claims, so a loss carried back could be wasted if it is set against income that is already covered by personal allowances.

Capital allowance claims are not all or nothing claims and the claim can be tailored to, say, preserve the personal allowance to prevent it being lost. A writing down allowance could, for example, be claimed in future years instead of claiming the annual investment allowance where this would increase a loss and waste the personal allowance.

Losses And Capital Allowances

Arthur is self-employed and makes a loss for 2022/23 of £25,000, including capital allowances of £8,000.

His taxable profit for the 2021/22 tax year was £30,000.

He wants to carry back the loss to 2021/22 but does not want to waste his personal allowance. By not claiming capital allowances, the loss is £17,000.

Carrying it back will reduce his profit for 2021/22 to £13,000, most of which will be sheltered by his personal allowance for the year of £12,570.

By not claiming capital allowances for 2022/23, he will have more capital allowances available in future years. Although he will not be able to claim the Annual Investment Allowance, he will be able to benefit from writing down allowances. By reducing the loss carried back, he also preserves the personal allowance in the previous year.

This means that he will save a considerable amount of tax in future years.

64. Unlisted Share Losses

Many people subscribe for shares in unlisted companies. These can include companies that your friends own.

A number of these companies will fail and, therefore, the original investment is lost.

Provided certain conditions are met (see HMRC Helpsheet HS286), allowable losses on these shares can be set against income rather than used as a capital loss. This is especially useful if you have no other gains during the year or are unlikely to make capital gains in the future.

Unlisted Share Losses

Louise subscribed for 1,000 shares in ABC Ltd, a company set up by her brother, and paid £10,000 for them. They are now worthless as the company has closed down. She is a higher rate taxpayer.

By claiming income tax relief on this capital loss, she recovers £4,000 of the loss. Had she claimed relief as a capital loss, she would only have recovered £2,000 of the loss.

65. Beware Cap On Income Tax Reliefs

A limit is placed on the amount that an individual may deduct by way of certain specified reliefs. The limit is set at £50,000 or 25% of the individual's adjusted total income for the tax year if this is greater. The reliefs subject to the limit include income tax loss reliefs, but not charitable donations and contributions to registered pension schemes.

Where reliefs available for the year exceed the limit, care should be taken to ensure that maximum relief is obtained subject to the cap, such as carrying back losses to the previous year or carrying trade losses forward, rather than relieving the loss in the current year. It is advisable that professional advice is sought.

Beware Cap On Income Tax Reliefs

Geoff has income of £180,000 in 2022/23. He makes a trading loss of £60,000. He prepares his accounts using the accruals basis. He has trading profits of £10,000 in 2021/22, £50,000 in 2020/21 and £40,000 in 2019/20.

Geoff wishes to set the loss against his general income of 2022/23. However, the relief available for that year is capped at £50,000, as this is greater than 25% of his income (£45,000). He can claim loss relief of £50,000 for 2022/23. He can carry the remaining £10,000 of the loss back against his trading profits of £10,000 for 2021/22, but will waste his personal allowance. Therefore, he will be better off carrying the remaining loss forward for relief against future profits.

66. Registering Your Capital Losses

If you bought an asset and sold it at a loss then it is possible that you made a capital loss (e.g. if you invested in a start-up that failed, bought shares that fell in value or bought an investment property which you subsequently sold for less than you paid for it, then this may well apply to you).

Capital losses can only be relieved against capital gains and if there are no gains in the year of the loss, the loss can be carried forward. However, if gains are incurred during the year that the loss was made, the loss is first set against the other gains for the year, with any balance remaining unused being carried forward. Losses must be set against gains of the same year before being carried forward, regardless of whether the gains exceed the annual exempt amount for capital gains tax (£12,300 for 2022/23 and remaining at this level for future years up to and including 2025/26).

In order to preserve a loss for use against gains in future years, it is necessary to establish that loss. You must report the loss in your tax return within four years or amend an already filed tax return to claim the loss. Alternatively, a claim can be made by writing to the tax inspector.

Remember, any size of loss if realised in isolation can be used in this way and could save you up to 20% (or 28% on residential property gains) tax on the amount of the loss in future years.

Therefore, always claim losses in the year in which they arise and keep a note of the amount of losses you have accumulated.

Registering Your Capital Losses

Simon sold some shares realising a significant loss of £20,000 in 2020/21 and had no other disposals in the year. He omitted to register the loss at the time.

He is planning on selling his investment residential property on which he will realise a significant capital gain. The sale will take place in 2022/23.

In order to utilise the loss on the shares, he submits a revised tax return for 2020/21 showing the capital loss, which is accepted by HMRC. The loss is carried forward to future years.

He can now use the loss against his capital gain in 2022/23, which as he is a higher rate taxpayer saves £5,600 in tax (£20,000 x 28%).

67. Registering Your Rental Losses

If you let out property, then you have an obligation to report the property income and expenses to HMRC (see www.gov.uk/renting-out-a-property/paying-tax) unless your rental income is less than £1,000 and you claim the property income allowance. Separate rules apply under the rent-a-room scheme if you let a furnished room in your own home.

You will need to tell HMRC that you are receiving income from property by 31 January after the end of the tax year in which the income is received. You may need to complete a tax return, in which case HMRC will notify you of the need to file a return. However, if you have PAYE earnings, you may be able to have any tax due collected via an adjustment to your PAYE code.

Even if you make a loss it is to your advantage to report this to HMRC. Many people do not realise this and only start reporting the income when they break into profit.

Without reporting the rental losses, you are losing out on being able to set these losses against future income from property, meaning that you may then pay more tax than you should.

So, if you register these losses now, you will be able to take them forward and offset them in future years.

Registering Your Rental Losses

Harry starts letting out a property in 2015/16

For each of the first five years, he calculates a loss of £1,000 per annum and declares this loss on his tax return.

Due to a rise in rental income from the property, he realises a profit of £1,500 in 2020/21, a profit of £2,000 in 2021/22 and a profit of £3,000 in 2022/23, which he also declares.

Because he has declared the losses in the previous five years, he is able to utilise the losses against the income and set them against the rental profits, saving tax on this income. He used £1,500 of the losses in 2020/21 to reduce the rental profit to nil, £2,000 of the losses in 2021/22 reducing the profit to nil, and the remaining £1,500 in 2022/23 reducing the rental profit to £1,500.

Assuming Harry pays tax at 40%, the total saved by using the losses is £2,000 (£5,000 x 40%).

Chapter 7:
Capital Allowances

68. Capital Allowances: Annual Investment Allowance

Ensuring that the annual investment allowance (AIA) is claimed on all new items of plant and machinery can save considerable amounts of tax and give immediate relief for capital expenditure against profits.

The AIA gives a 100% deduction against profits up to the amount of the allowance. The permanent level of the allowance is set at £200,000. However, a temporary limit of £1 million applies for the period from 1 January 2019 to 31 March 2023.

Where the chargeable accounting period spans a date on which the level of the allowance changes, transitional rules apply (see Tip 70). Particular care must be taken where the period spans 31 March 2023.

As the window in which to benefit from the higher AIA is limited, businesses may wish to consider accelerating capital expenditure to take advantage of the immediate write-off that the AIA offers, where this is likely to be beneficial.

In certain circumstances, it can be more beneficial to claim the writing down allowance rather than the AIA, for example, to preserve personal allowances.

Claiming the writing down allowance may also be preferable if the intention is to dispose of the asset after a short period of time, so as to minimise balancing charges on the disposal.

Note: companies also have the option of claiming the super-deduction for expenditure incurred in the period from 1 April 2021 to 31 March 2023 (see Tip 71). Where this is available, this will be more advantageous that the AIA, as it gives a deduction for 130% of the expenditure rather than 100%.

Capital Allowances: Annual Investment Allowance

Paul is a sole trader. He prepares accounts to 31 March each year. In the year to 31 March 2023, he purchases a new van costing £22,000.

He claims the AIA and is able to receive full and immediate relief for the expenditure in working out his taxable profits for the year to 31 March 2023, assessable in 2022/23.

69. Annual Investment Allowance: Take Advantage Of The Temporary Increase

The annual investment allowance (AIA) is temporarily increased to £1 million for the period from 1 January 2019 to 31 March 2023. The allowance will revert to its permanent level of £200,000 from 1 April 2023. Where a chargeable accounting period falls wholly within the period from 1 January 2019 to 31 March 2023, the AIA is £1 million (proportionately reduced where the chargeable period is less than 12 months). Where the period spanned 1 January 2019 or spans 31 March 2023, transitional rules apply (see Tip 70).

Where larger capital projects are on the agenda, consider timing the expenditure to take advantage of the temporary increase in the AIA and achieve relief for expenditure sooner.

Note: companies also have the option of claiming the super-deduction for expenditure incurred in the period from 1 April 2021 to 31 March 2023 (see Tip 71). Where this is available, this will be more advantageous that the AIA, as it gives a deduction for 130% of the expenditure rather than 100%.

Annual Investment Allowance: Take Advantage Of The Temporary Increase

John is a sole trader. He prepares accounts to 31 March each year. He is planning significant investment in plant and machinery. In order to benefit from the higher AIA limit, he purchases £250,000 of machinery in March 2023.

John is able to take advantage of the higher AIA limit and claim the AIA for the full amount of the expenditure. Had he delayed the investment until the following year, he would have only been able to claim the AIA for £200,000 of the expenditure. Relief for the remaining £50,000 would have been given in the form of writing down allowances. Claiming the AIA provides John with immediate relief for the expenditure against his taxable profits.

70. Beware Chargeable Accounting Periods Spanning 31 March 2023

As noted in Tips 68 and 69, the annual investment allowance (AIA) is temporarily increased to £1 million for the period from 1 January 2019 to 31 March 2023. However, transitional rules apply where the chargeable accounting period spans 1 January 2019 or 31 March 2023. The transitional rules can catch the unwary. The AIA reverts to £200,000 from 1 April 2023.

Where the chargeable period spans 31 March 2023 it is split into two parts – the period up to and including 31 March 2023 and the period from 1 April 2023 onwards.

The AIA for periods spanning 31 March 2023is the sum of:

- the AIA entitlement for the period up to and including 31 March 2023 based on the cap of £1 million applying to that period; and
- the AIA entitlement for the period on or after 1 April 2023 based on the cap of £200,000 applying to that period.

However, a further cap equal to the AIA entitlement for the period on or after 1 April 2023 applies to expenditure incurred on or after that date (rather than capping it at £200,000 as was the case for pre-1 January 2019 expenditure where the accounting period spanned 1 January 2019).

This can seriously restrict the available AIA where expenditure is incurred after 31 March 2023 in a period spanning that date, denying relief even where the expenditure is less than the AIA limit for the period as a whole.

Note: companies also have the option of claiming the super-deduction for expenditure incurred in the period from 1 April 2021 to 31 March 2023 (see Tip 71). Where this is available, this will be more advantageous that the AIA, as it gives a deduction for 130% of the expenditure rather than 100%.

Beware Chargeable Accounting Periods Spanning 31 March 2023

Hamish runs an unincorporated business. He is planning to invest £750,000 in new equipment in the next two years. He prepares accounts to 30 April each year.

For the year to 30 April 2023, the transitional rules apply in working out the AIA limit, as the period spans 31 March 2023. The AIA for the period is £933,333 ((11/12 x £1 million) + (1/12 x £200,000)). However, a further cap of £16,667 applies to any expenditure incurred on or after 1 April 2023 (this is the AIA for the period 1 April 2023 to 30 April 2023, being 1/12 x £200,000).

Therefore, as long as Hamish incurs the expenditure of £750,000 before 1 April 2023, he can claim the AIA for the full amount as the qualifying expenditure is less than the AIA limit for the period. However, if Hamish incurs the expenditure in April 2023, he will only be able to claim the AIA for £16,667 of the expenditure, claiming WDAs for the balance of £733,333.

71. Take Advantage Of The Super-Deduction Available To Companies

For a limited period, companies are able to benefit from a super-deduction equal to 130% of qualifying expenditure. The super-deduction is not available to unincorporated businesses, such as sole traders and partnerships.

The super-deduction is available in respect of qualifying expenditure on new and unused assets that would otherwise be eligible for main rate (18%) writing down allowances. To qualify, the expenditure must be incurred in the two-year period from 1 April 2021 to 31 March 2023. Expenditure on new computer equipment, office furniture, vans, lorries and machinery may qualify for the super-deduction. However, the super-deduction is not available for expenditure on cars.

Claiming the super-deduction will provide a greater reduction in profits than can be achieved by claiming the annual investment allowance (AIA).

A balancing charge will apply when the asset is sold. The calculation of the balancing charge will depend on the date on which the asset is sold.

Take Advantage Of The Super-Deduction Available To Companies

X Ltd is planning on investing in new and unused plant and machinery to boost their business as it recovers from the impact of the Covid-19 pandemic. They plan to spend £500,000 in

September 2022. The expenditure would qualify for main rate writing down allowances at the rate of 18%.

The company prepares accounts to 31 March each year.

The company has a number of options available to it as regards securing relief for its capital expenditure.

As the expenditure is eligible for the super-deduction, the company could claim the super-deduction, which would reduce taxable profits for the year by £650,000 (£500,000 x 130%). This would generate a corporation tax saving of £123,500 (£650,000 @ 19%).

This is more beneficial than claiming the AIA, which would reduce profits by £500,000, saving corporation tax of £95,000 (£500,000 @19%). The AIA limit for the year to 31 March 2023 is £1 million.

72. Claim The 50% FYA For Companies

The super-deduction (see Tip 71) is only available for qualifying expenditure by companies on new and unused assets incurred between 1 April 2021 and 31 March 2023 which would qualify for main rate writing down allowances. Expenditure on new and unused assets in the same period that would qualify for special rate allowances, as would be the case for long-life assets, thermal insulation and integral features, is able to benefit from a 50% first-year allowance (FYA). The FYA is not available for cars.

As with the super-deduction, only companies can benefit.

The FYA offers a lower rate of deduction (at 50%) than that available where the annual investment allowance (AIA) is claimed (at 100%). However, where the AIA has been used up, the FYA provides an opportunity to secure immediate write-off of 50% of the expenditure against profits – a more attractive option than a writing down allowance (WDA) of 6%.

Claim The 50% FYA For Companies

Y Ltd prepares accounts to 31 March each year. They have already used up their AIA limit for the year to 31 March 2023.

They plan to incur qualifying expenditure on new thermal insulation in February 2023. The thermal insulation will cost £2 million.

They claim the 50% FYA, receiving relief for £1 million in calculating their taxable profits for the year to 31 March 2023. The remaining £1 million is allocated to the special rate pool and writing down allowances are claimed at the rate of 6%.

By claiming the 50% FYA they will save tax of £190,000 plus a further £11,400 by virtue of the WDA claimed on the balance – a total saving of £201,400 for the year to 31 March 2023. Had they only claimed the WDA, they would have reduced their tax bill by only £22,800.

73. Short Life Assets

You can treat capital items that you expect to keep for no more than eight years from the end of the accounting period in which you acquired them as short life assets by making a relevant election.

Where this election is made, the asset is not added to the general capital allowances pool. This means that if it is disposed of within the eight-year period, any loss arising on the scrapping or sale will be realised straight away rather than affecting the general pool.

If the asset is still held after the end of the eight-year period, it is automatically added back into the general pool.

Short Life Assets

Graham buys £10,000 worth of new equipment which he thinks will last less than eight years and hence elects to treat it as a short life asset.

After three years he is proved right when the equipment has passed its useful life and is scrapped, at which point he can claim a balancing allowance for the remainder of his original cost against his profits.

74. Write Off Small Pools

The small pools allowance allows you to write off the main or special rate pool, or both, if the balance on the pool in question is £1,000 or less. This clears the pool in one hit and prevents the need to make minimal capital allowance claims over a number of years.

The small pools allowance can be claimed in respect of new expenditure (usually that remaining after other allowances have been claimed), any brought forward residual balance, less any disposal proceeds of assets which have been sold or otherwise disposed of.

The £1,000 small pools allowance is proportionately reduced for periods of less than 12 months.

Write Off Small Pools
Helen has a balance of £800 on her main pool.
As the balance on the pool is less than £1,000, Helen claims the small pools allowance, claiming a writing down allowance for the full £800.
The balance on the main pool is reduced to nil.

75. Zero Emission Cars And 100% FYA

The annual investment allowance is not available in respect of cars. Likewise, expenditure on cars does not qualify for the super-deduction (see Tip 71) or the 50% first-year allowance (see Tip 72) available to companies. However, it is still possible to obtain a 100% deduction against profits for a car purchased for your business by choosing an electric car. New zero emission cars purchased on or after 1 April 2021 qualify for the 100% first-year allowance (FYA).

Zero Emission Cars And 100% Allowance

Ben has a small family business and is looking to buy a company car.

In May 2022, he chooses a new electric car which costs £15,000.

As the car's CO2 emissions are zero, he can claim a 100% FYA thereby obtaining an immediate write-off against profits of £15,000.

As the rate of corporation tax is 19% for the financial year 2022, claiming the 100% FYA will reduce his tax bill by £2,850 (£15,000 @ 19%).

Had he spent £15,000 on a car which did not qualify for the FYA but only for an 18% WDA, his tax bill would have been reduced by £513 in that year (19% of (£15,000 @ 18%)).

By choosing a zero emission car and claiming the FYA, he is able to write off the cost immediately and increase his tax saving by £2,337 (compared to claiming only a writing down allowance) in that year.

However, in subsequent years he will pay slightly more tax as he will not be able to claim a WDA.

Choosing an electric car also keeps the benefit-in-kind tax that Ben will pay on his company car low. For 2022/23, the appropriate percentage for a zero emission car is only 2% (see Tip 43).

76. Time Your Capital Expenditure

If your cash flow allows it, carefully consider the date on which you invest in new items of plant and machinery or other items qualifying for capital allowances. A purchase date of a few days either side of your accounting year-end date can make a difference of 12 months in when the relief is obtained. Moving the purchase date from one side of the year-end into a new accounting period will delay relief for that expenditure by one year. The timing of capital expenditure is also particularly important in qualifying for time-limited reliefs, such as the temporary increase in the annual investment allowance (AIA), particularly where the transitional rules apply (see Tips 68, 69 and 70) and for companies, access to the super-deduction and the 50% first-year allowance (see Tips 71 and 72).

Time Your Capital Expenditure

Gordon is considering buying £10,000 worth of equipment for his unincorporated business. His year-end is 31 March.

By making the purchase prior to the accounting year-end date, he will be able to claim allowances (either the annual investment allowance or the writing down allowance) a year earlier than if he delayed the purchase until a few days after the year-end. If he purchases the item on 27 March 2023, relief will be given for the year to 31 March 2023 (assessable in 2022/23), whereas if he purchases the item on 3 April 2023, relief for the expenditure will be given for the year to 31 March 2024 (assessable in 2023/24).

By advancing the purchase by a few days, he will receive the tax relief a year earlier.

Chapter 8:
VAT

77. Should I Register For VAT Voluntarily?

78. The VAT Cash Accounting Scheme

79. Is The VAT Flat Rate Scheme For Small Businesses Beneficial?

77. Should I Register For VAT Voluntarily?

If your taxable turnover is below the VAT threshold then you may not have considered whether registering for VAT could be advantageous for you. The VAT registration threshold is £85,000 and will remain at this level until 31 March 2024.

If you incur VAT on supplies and the majority of your customers are registered for VAT, then it may be beneficial to register for VAT on a voluntary basis.

This will allow you to recover the input tax paid on the supplies and also allow you to charge VAT on your invoices.

It will also be beneficial if many of your sales are zero-rated, such as food, as you will be able to reclaim VAT suffered and may receive a VAT repayment each quarter, which is beneficial from a cash flow perspective.

If you decide to register for VAT, then your VAT-registered customers will be able to recover the VAT charged on your invoices when they next submit their VAT return.

VAT-registered businesses with VATable turnover below the VAT registration threshold who have not joined Making Tax Digital (MTD) for VAT voluntarily, must do so from the start of their first VAT accounting period which begins on or after 1 April 2022.

Should I Register For VAT Voluntarily?

Mark supplies parts to various garages, all of which are registered for VAT. His taxable turnover is around £60,000 a year.

He pays input tax on all his supplies and hence would be considerably better off by voluntarily registering for VAT and recovering this input tax.

By registering for VAT, he will also need to charge output tax on his sales.

He will also need to comply with the requirements of MTD for VAT.

78. The VAT Cash Accounting Scheme

If your VAT-exclusive turnover is £1.35m or less, then you may account for and pay VAT on the basis of cash paid and received.

You can join this scheme at any time.

Once you are in the scheme you can continue to use it until your taxable turnover exceeds £1.6 million per annum.

Joining the cash accounting scheme means that you don't have to pay VAT to HMRC on invoices that have not been paid yet and conversely are not allowed to claim VAT back on expenses you have incurred but not yet paid.

The VAT Cash Accounting Scheme

Paul uses the cash accounting scheme as his turnover is below £1.35 million per annum.

His major customer is having cash flow difficulties and, as a result, he does not pay Paul for his invoices totalling £100,000 (net) until nine months after the invoice date, at which time Paul accounts to HMRC for the VAT due on these.

If Paul was not using the cash accounting scheme, he would have had to account for VAT on an invoice basis and would, therefore, have been out of pocket to the tune of £20,000 for a period of up to nine months.

Businesses may fail if they do not have sufficient cash to pay this debt or bank facilities to fund the VAT due. The cash accounting scheme removes this risk.

79. Is The VAT Flat Rate Scheme For Small Businesses Beneficial?

If you are a small business, it can be advantageous to join the VAT flat rate scheme for small businesses.

Under the scheme, you use a flat rate percentage to work out the amount of VAT you need to pay over to HMRC. You do not need to record VAT on sales and purchases separately and claim the difference. This can save a lot of work.

The flat rate percentage depends on your business sector. The percentages are listed on the GOV.UK website (see the guidance at www.gov.uk/vat-flat-rate-scheme/how-much-you-pay). The input tax payable to HMRC is worked out by multiplying the flat rate percentage for the relevant business sector by turnover for the quarter inclusive of VAT.

You can join the scheme as long as your turnover excluding VAT is not more than £150,000 a year. You can stay in the scheme until your turnover reaches £230,000 a year.

However, if you are classed as a 'limited cost trader' the scheme may not be beneficial for you, particularly if you incur VAT on services and other goods not taken into account in determining whether a trader is a limited costs trader. The flat rate percentage for limited cost traders is 16.5% of VAT-inclusive turnover – equivalent to 19.8% of net turnover, allowing only a very narrow margin to cover input VAT.

More details on the scheme can be found in HMRC Notice 733.

Is The VAT Flat Rate Scheme For Small Businesses Beneficial?

Gill runs a computer repair business. Her annual turnover excluding VAT is £100,000. She registers for the VAT flat rate scheme.

In a particular VAT quarter, her turnover, including VAT, is £31,200. The flat rate percentage for her sector is 10.5%.

She must pay VAT of £3,276 (10.5% x £31,200) over to HMRC.

Chapter 9:
Capital Gains Tax

80. Timing Your Disposals For CGT

A timing advantage of one year on the payment of capital gains tax can be achieved simply by delaying disposal beyond 5 April in the tax year, so that you have use of the funds for another year and can earn interest on this money for a year longer before having to pay the tax to HMRC. However, this is not an option where the gain relates to the disposal of a UK residential property as a payment on account of the capital gains tax due must be made within 60 days of completion where a chargeable gain arises on the sale of a residential property. You must also report the associated gain to HMRC within the same time frame.

However, it can also be advantageous to accelerate a disposal so that it takes place before the end of the tax year if you have not used the annual exemption for that year, and the gain on the planned disposal would be covered by the annual exemption; in this situation it is beneficial to make the disposal before the end of the tax year.

Likewise, if you have already realised gains in excess of the annual exempt amount and are planning on selling an asset that will realise a loss, accelerating the disposal so that it takes place before the end of the tax year will mean that the loss is available to set against gains, reducing the tax payable. However, when deciding whether this is worthwhile, consideration should be given to whether any of the annual exempt amount is wasted, and whether it would be better to dispose of the asset in the new tax year to benefit from both the annual exemption and the loss in full.

Timing Your Disposals For CGT

Jack is considering selling some shares in March or April 2023. He has already realised gains in 2022/23 in excess of his annual exemption of £12,300. The sale would generate a gain of around £40,000. By delaying the sale until after 5 April 2023, he will pay tax on the gain a year later than if he sells the shares on or before 5 April 2023 and will have the 2023/24 exempt amount available to reduce the chargeable gain. He also has the opportunity to earn some interest on the money he has put aside for his tax liability.

81. Transfer Assets To Your Spouse Or Civil Partner

Spouses and civil partners are able to transfer assets between them at a value that gives rise to neither a gain nor a loss. This means that no capital gains tax liability arises where assets are transferred between them. This can be useful from a tax planning perspective, reducing the couple's combined capital gains tax bill. The transferee simply assumes the transferor's base cost.

Transferring an asset before sale can access a spouse's or partner's unused annual exempt amount (see Tip 5) or reduce the rate at which the gain is taxed.

However, it should be noted that in doing this, the capital gains tax liability is transferred to the spouse/civil partner. This is something that they should be happy to accept before proceeding with the transfer. The recipient will also benefit from the net sale proceeds.

Transfer Assets To Your Spouse Or Civil Partner

Adam and Jake are in a civil partnership. Both have used their annual exempt amount for 2022/23.

Adam wishes to sell some further shares to fund the renovation of their kitchen. The sale will generate a chargeable gain of £24,000.

Adam is a higher rate taxpayer and Jake is a basic rate taxpayer.

If Adam simply sells the shares, the gain will be taxed at 20%. He will pay tax of £4,800, leaving him with net sale proceeds of £19,200.

However, if the couple take advantage of the no gain/no loss rule to transfer the shares to Jake prior to the sale, Jake will realise the gain of £24,000, on which, as a basic rate taxpayer, he will pay tax at 10%. Consequently, he will only pay tax of £2,400, leaving him with net sale proceeds of £21,600.

By transferring the shares prior to sale, the couple have an additional £2,400 to spend on their kitchen renovation.

82. Roll-Over Relief For Business Assets

When selling certain types of business asset, it may be possible to postpone the gain by reinvesting in a qualifying asset for roll-over relief purposes. This is quite a restricted relief and care should be taken that the qualifying conditions are met before relying on the availability of the relief.

The relief is available where proceeds from the disposal of qualifying business assets are used wholly or in part to buy new assets. The new assets must be bought within the period running from one year before the disposal of the old asset to three years after the disposal. The business must be trading both when the old assets are disposed of and the new assets are acquired, and both the old asset and the new asset must be used in the business. The effect of the relief is to reduce the base cost of the new asset by the gain on the disposal of the old asset, delaying the time at which the gain on the old asset is brought into charge until the new asset is sold. Relief is available for land and buildings and fixed plant and machinery.

Further information on Business Asset Roll-over Relief can be found in HMRC Helpsheet HS290.

Roll-Over Relief For Business Assets

Martin sells a qualifying business asset for £100,000, making a gain of £50,000.

He reinvests the entire proceeds into a new qualifying asset, costing £120,000 and the gain is entirely rolled over into the new asset.

The base cost of the new asset is reduced by the rolled-over gain of £50,000 to £70,000 (£120,000 – £50,000). However, there is no capital gains tax to pay when the old asset is sold – the capital gains tax payable on the sale of the old asset is postponed until the sale of the new asset. This creates a cash flow advantage as Martin does not need to keep back some of the proceeds to pay capital gains tax and can invest the full amount of the proceeds in the new asset.

83. Make A Negligible Value Claim For Worthless Assets

If you own an asset or shares that have become worthless you can make a claim to treat the asset as if you had sold it and immediately reacquired it at the time of the claim for its value at that time. The claim, known as a negligible value claim, enables relief to be given for the loss in value of the asset.

The loss is treated as arising in the year in which the claim is made, or at a time specified in the claim in the two preceding tax years during which time the conditions for the claim were met.

Make A Negligible Value Claim For Worthless Assets

Karen purchased a painting which cost £10,000. In June 2022, the painting is found to be a worthless fake.

Karen makes a negligible value claim for 2022/23 for the loss on the painting of £10,000. The loss will, in the first instance, be set against any capital gains for 2022/23. If it has not been fully used in 2022/23, any balance is carried forward against future capital gains. Making the claim could save Karen capital gains tax of £2,000 if she is a higher rate taxpayer (or more if set against a residential property gain).

Chapter 10:
Property

84. Utilise Rent-A-Room Relief

If you let out furnished accommodation within a property in which you live, then you can earn up to £7,500 in tax-free rent in 2022/23. If the rental income is shared between two or more people, each has a limit of £3,750 – regardless of the number of people benefitting from the rental income.

The exemption is automatic if the rental income is less than the threshold and does not need to be declared to HMRC.

Where rental income exceeds the rent-a-room limit, there are various options. The taxpayer can choose to use the scheme and work out the taxable profits by deducting the rent-a-room limit. This may be beneficial if expenses are less than the rent-a-room limit.

However, if there is a loss, it may be beneficial not to use rent-a-room, but instead calculate the actual loss so as to retain the benefit of the loss.

Utilise Rent-A-Room Relief

Scenario 1 – When it is beneficial to use the relief

Matthew, a higher rate taxpayer, rents out a room in his house for £4,250 per annum, incurring £1,250 in the way of costs. He claims rent-a-room relief for 2022/23 and pays no tax on the rent he received. Had he not claimed the relief he would have paid tax at 40% on rental profits of £3,000 (£4,250 – £1,250). By claiming the relief, he saves himself £1,200 in tax.

Scenario 2 – When it is not beneficial to use the relief

Luke rents out a room and, after expenses, makes a loss of £1,000, as the rental income is £9,000 and his expenses are £10,000.

Clearly he is better off not making the election, as to do so would turn his £1,000 loss into a profit of £1,500 (£9,000 − £7,500) on which he would incur tax; under the rent-a-room scheme where income exceeds the £7,500 limit, the excess over the limit is taxed (without regard to the expenses).

85. Furnished Holiday Lettings

Furnished holiday lettings offer tax advantages over other types of lettings. This is because a furnished holiday business is treated like a trade rather than an investment business.

As all UK furnished holiday lets by the same person are treated as part of the same FHL business, losses on one property are effectively offset against profits from other properties in the same year. Losses are not restricted to set off against the same property, just the same FHL business. Losses arising from a furnished holiday lettings business as a whole can only be set off against profits from the same furnished holiday lettings business.

As furnished holiday lettings are treated like a trade, they benefit from some advantages compared to other lettings. Capital allowances may be claimed in respect of plant and machinery. Capital gains tax reliefs, such as business asset disposal relief and roll-over relief may also be available.

However, to qualify as a furnished holiday letting and to benefit from associated advantages, the property must be let as a furnished holiday let for 105 days in the tax year and must be available for letting for 210 days in the tax year. Lettings of 31 days or more do not count in satisfying these tests.

Where this test is not met in a particular year, there are ways in which this can be overcome. If a landlord has more than one furnished holiday lettings property, an averaging election can be made to apply the test by virtue of the average occupancy over all the properties let by the landlord as furnished holiday lettings. This may be useful where some properties are year-round lets and others are only occupied in the summer season.

A period of grace election can be made if a property fails to meet the FHL occupancy condition for a year despite a genuine intention to let, provided that the occupancy condition was met in the previous year (either on its own or as the result of an averaging). Making an election allows the property to remain within the regime for one or two years. This is worthwhile as it allows time to increase the letting without having to deal with the consequences of becoming a non-holiday let (such as possible balancing charges). If the property does not meet the required letting level in the fourth year (after being treated as qualifying for two years), it is no longer treated as a FHL.

Where a property is let on short-term lets, the FHL rules offer advantages over other lets. It is still worthwhile to fall within the FHL regime.

Furnished Holiday Lettings

Heath buys a house in Padstow, which qualifies as a furnished holiday letting. He also has properties which are let as holiday lets in Edinburgh and Whitstable. In 2022/23, he fails to meet the occupancy test for the Edinburgh property. However, on average, the properties are let as holiday lets for 125 days in the year. By making an averaging election, the occupancy condition is met and all three properties qualify as furnished holiday lettings.

He plans to sell the Edinburgh property and reinvest the proceeds in a holiday let in Norfolk.

He will be able to benefit from the capital gains tax reliefs available to traders, such as roll-over relief.

86. Claim The Property Income Allowance

The property income allowance allows an individual to enjoy property income of up to £1,000 tax-free without having to declare it to HMRC.

Where property income exceeds £1,000, the individual has the option of deducting the allowance rather than actual expenses and paying tax on the excess. This would be beneficial if the actual expenses are less than £1,000.

If property income is less than £1,000 and expenses exceed the income so that there is a loss, claiming the allowance will not be beneficial as the loss will be wasted. A loss cannot be claimed where the property allowance is used. However, if the individual is unlikely to utilise the loss in the future (for example, if the property income is a one-off), it may be simpler to take advantage of the allowance and not report it to HMRC.

Claim The Property Income Allowance
Alan lives near a major racecourse and lets out his drive for parking. He makes about £500 a year.
He takes advantage of the property income allowance to enjoy the income tax-free without reporting it to HMRC.

87. Claim Relief For Replacement Domestic Items

If you let a property furnished, you cannot obtain relief for the initial cost of domestic items. However, you can claim relief for the cost of replacement items. The relief is limited to the cost of an equivalent replacement, plus costs of acquisition and disposal. Where the replacement is superior (for example, replacing a fridge with a fridge-freezer) the deduction is capped at the cost of the item equivalent to that being replaced.

The cost of the replacement is simply deducted in working out the profits of the property rental business.

> ### Claim Relief For Replacement Domestic Items
>
> Karen has let a property furnished for many years. In 2022/23 she receives rents of £15,000.
>
> She replaces the curtains in the property at a cost of £1,000. She also incurs a delivery fee of £20.
>
> She claims a deduction for £1,020, being the cost of the replacement curtains and the delivery charge.
>
> If she had sold the old curtains, any sale proceeds would have to be taken into account in calculating the profit.

88. Principal Private Residence Relief

Most people are aware of this relief, which allows you to sell your home without having to pay capital gains tax on any profit that you make.

There are many rules associated with this relief, but it is a very valuable exemption as, for the majority of people, the purchase of their home is the biggest investment they ever make.

Where you own more than one home, you can choose which one is your main residence, as long as you are living in the property selected as a home. By changing the appropriate election (often known as flipping), it is possible to maximise the benefit of the relief (see Tip 89). Professional advice should be sought prior to making an election.

Principal Private Residence Relief

Harry sells his house in October 2022 for £650,000, having purchased the property in May 2012 for £375,000. As it has been his only or main residence throughout his ownership, he qualifies for principal private residence relief and no tax is payable on the gain he has made on the sale of the property.

As the gain is entirely sheltered by principal private residence relief, he does not need to report the gain to HMRC within 60 days of completion.

89. Choosing Your Main Residence

Where you have more than one property that you live in as a home, it is possible to choose which property is your main residence for private residence relief purposes at any given time, provided the elected property is used as a home. However, a person can only have one main residence at any one time. Spouses and civil partners can only have one main residence between them.

By 'flipping' the properties, it is possible to maximise relief and ensure that the final periods for each property qualify for relief (see Tip 90).

Choosing Your Main Residence

Harvey has a flat in the city that he bought for £500,000 in April 2012. In April 2014, he buys a family home in the country for £800,000. He lives in the flat in the week and the country home at weekends and during holidays.

He immediately elects for the country home to be his main residence.

He sells the country home in July 2022 for £1,200,000, buying a larger property nearby. As the property has been his main residence throughout, the gain is tax-free.

He also sells the flat in July 2022 to fund the purchase of a larger property as his new home, making a gain of £150,000. He is able to claim principal private residence relief in respect of the periods from April 2012 to April 2014 and also for the last nine months.

Had John not flipped his properties so that his country home was his main residence, he would not have been entitled to principal private residence relief on the sale and the gain of £400,000 would have attracted capital gains tax at the higher rates applying to residential property gains.

Although some of the gain on the flat is taxable, the overall tax bill is much reduced. He is also able to shelter the last nine months of the gain arising on both properties (see Tip 90).

90. The Final Period Exemption

If a property has been your principal private residence at some point during the period that you have owned it, then the final period of ownership is exempt from capital gains tax. The exemption for the final period is nine months where the disposal took place on or after 6 April 2020. However, where the owner or their spouse or civil partner is disabled or one of the couple has moved into a residential care home, the final period exemption is 36 months.

The final period exemption applies if you have lived in the property at some point as your only or main residence; it does not have to be your only or main residence when it's sold. Where two properties (or more) are owned, taking advantage of flipping enables each property to be the main residence at some point so that each property benefits from the final period exemption.

The Final Period Exemption

Tom sells a property in January 2023. He has owned the property for ten years. He lived in it as his main residence for five years and kept it as a second home for the remaining five years.

He realises a gain on sale of £100,000.

He owned the property for 120 months, 60 of which the property was his main residence. As it has been a main residence, the final nine months will qualify for principal private residence relief – a total of 69 months. Consequently, 69/120 of the gain (£57,500) qualifies for principal private residence relief. The taxable gain is therefore £42,500 (£100,000 – £57,500).

91. Private Lettings Relief: Shared Occupancy

The availability of lettings relief was seriously curtailed in relation to disposals on or after 6 April 2020 and is nowhere near as valuable a relief as it once was. However, it is still available where the landlord shares occupancy of the property with the tenant.

Where the conditions are met, lettings relief is the lower of the following amounts:

* the private residence available on the disposal;

* the gain attributable to the letting; and

* £40,000.

Private Lettings Relief: Shared Occupancy

Since buying his home, Richard has let out the top floor, comprising two rooms and bathroom, to tenants and continues to occupy the property as a home.

In August 2022, he sells the property realising a gain of £200,000. The let area comprises 30% of the property. Therefore, only 70% of the gain is eligible for principal private residence relief. The principal private residence relief is worth £140,000.

The remaining gain, £60,000, is attributable to the letting.

As Richard has occupied the property with his tenants as his home, he qualifies for lettings relief. The lettings relief is the lower of:

* £140,000 (gain qualifying for private residence relief);

- £60,000 (gain attributable to letting); and

- £40,000.

Thus, lettings relief is £40,000 and the exempt gain is £180,000 (principal private residence relief of £140,000 and lettings relief of £40,000). The remaining gain of £20,000 is chargeable. To the extent that it is not sheltered by the annual exempt amount it is taxable at the residential property gain rates.

Richard must report the gain to HMRC within 60 days of the date of completion and pay tax on account of the gain within the same time frame.

Chapter 11:
Inheritance Tax

92. IHT And Gifts Out Of Income

There is an exemption for inheritance tax purposes, in addition to the £3,000 annual allowance, for gifts made out of income on a regular basis. This can be a very useful exemption where someone is looking to minimise inheritance tax on their estate and has surplus income. Where gifts are made out of income, there is no inheritance tax – the donor does not need to survive seven years for the gift to fall out of charge as in the case of a PET (see Tip 94).

It is important to establish the regularity of the payments in order to qualify for this relief, so if gifts are made in cash then these should be regular in amount and frequency, taking one year with another. Use could be made of this relief, for example, by a grandparent paying for a grandchild's school fees or meeting a regular household expense for an adult child. Alternatively, a standing order could be set up to make a regular gift from income.

Another way of establishing regular payments may be to take out an investment policy for someone such as your (adult) child, with premiums being due on a regular basis.

IHT And Gifts Out Of Income

Walter is 60 and earns £200,000 per year.

He has a son who is 25, who cannot work at present due to ill health.

Walter, who does not need the majority of his income, wishes to gift his son £50,000 per year, but is worried about the effects this will have on his inheritance tax bill should he not survive the seven years necessary for these monies to drop out of his estate.

He establishes a quarterly standing order into his son's account and writes a letter to his son stating that he intends to gift this amount per annum for as long as he continues to work.

93. Make A Will

Surprisingly, many people still die intestate (i.e. without a will).

With the ease that wills can now be drafted and the low cost of such services, it makes good sense to make a will and it can save a lot of needless heartache and stress for those left behind, not to mention saving a lot of tax.

A simple will gifting all your worldly goods to your spouse or civil partner will avoid IHT on your entire estate, as gifts between spouses/civil partners are exempt from IHT if the spouse or partner is UK domiciled.

Remember, if the nil rate band is not fully used on the first death, the unused percentage is available on the death of the deceased's spouse/civil partner. The same applies to the residence nil rate band.

Make A Will

Rudolph dies intestate in April 2022, leaving an estate valued at £2.25 million. His wife receives £1.25 million (£250,000 plus half the remainder) and his children receive the remaining £1 million. As the proportion of the estate left to his children exceeds the nil rate band of £325,000, his family will face a hefty inheritance tax bill. This could easily have been avoided by making a will and leaving all his estate to his spouse or leaving assets to his children up to the nil rate band (£325,000) and the remainder to his spouse.

94. Potentially Exempt Transfers

Inheritance tax (IHT) can be mitigated by proper planning.

One of the most useful tools is the potentially exempt transfer (PET).

Under the PET rules, any gift made to an individual is exempt from inheritance tax if the donor survives seven years from the date of the gift. If the donor dies before seven years have elapsed, the amount charged to tax is calculated on a sliding scale, with a lower amount being taxed the longer that the donor survives after making the gift. It is also possible to protect against the IHT liability in the interim period by taking out decreasing term assurance, which basically covers the reducing IHT liability over the seven years.

Potentially Exempt Transfers

Gerald makes PETs to his children, Lucy and Lauren, of £250,000 each on 2 October 2015.

Provided he survives until 2 October 2022, these gifts will drop out of his estate and he will have saved his estate from paying inheritance tax of up to £200,000 (40% of £500,000) on this money.

Chapter 12:
Tax Returns and Administration

95. File Your Tax Return By 30 December

96. File Your Tax Return On Time To Avoid Hefty Penalties

97. Avoid Unnecessary Interest

98. Check Your Tax Code?

99. Payments On Account

100. Watch Out For The Online Tax Calculation...

95. File Your Tax Return By 30 December

Although you have until 31 January after the end of the tax year to file your tax return, if you file it online by 30 December and the amount of tax that you owe is less than £3,000, you can have the tax you owe collected through your PAYE code, rather than having to pay it in one go by 31 January.

This has considerable cash flow advantages.

File Your Tax Return By 30 December

Adam files his tax return online on 15 December. He pays tax at 40%. He owes tax of £1,800 and chooses to have the tax collected through his PAYE code. This delays payment, spreading it throughout the following tax year and saving him from having to make a payment of £1,800 by 31 January.

96. File Your Tax Return On Time To Avoid Hefty Penalties

Hefty penalties apply to people who fail to file their tax return on time and you could pay as much as £1,300 in penalties if you file your tax return six months late.

The longer the delay in filing the return, the higher the penalty that is charged. Paper returns for 2021/22 must be filed by 31 October 2022 and online returns must be filed by 31 January 2023. Paper returns for 2022/23 must be filed by 31 October 2023 and online returns by 31 January 2024.

Where a return is filed after these dates, a penalty is charged. The penalty is £100 if the return is filed one day late, even if you do not owe any tax. If the return is filed up to three months late, a further penalty of £10 per day is charged, up to a maximum of £900. If the return is filed six months late, a further penalty of £300 or 5% of the tax due, if higher, is charged.

A further penalty of £300 or 5% of the tax due, if higher, is charged if the return is still outstanding after 12 months.

File Your Tax Return On Time To Avoid Hefty Penalties

John files his 2020/21 self-assessment return online on 10 August 2022. The return was due by 31 January 2022 (although HMRC waived the automatic £100 late filing fee if the return was filed by midnight on 28 February 2022). The tax due was £1,000. John is charged a penalty of £100 for failing to file the return by midnight on 28 February 2022. The return is still outstanding on 1 May, so John is charged daily penalties of £10 per day for 90 days – a further

£900. As the return is still outstanding six months after the due date of 31 January 2022, John is charged a further penalty of £300. In total, not filing his return until 10 August 2022 costs him £1,300 in penalties. The penalties could easily have been avoided had John been more organised and filed his return by the extended deadline of 28 February 2022.

The penalties apply in addition to interest and surcharges on late paid tax.

97. Avoid Unnecessary Interest

By ensuring that you pay any tax on time, you can avoid paying HMRC non-deductible interest for the late payment of tax.

If you are likely to struggle to pay your tax, it is advisable to try and agree a Time-to-Pay agreement in advance with HMRC. While interest will still accrue, this can save much stress as a manageable payment plan can be agreed with HMRC.

Avoid Unnecessary Interest

Peter files his 2020/21 tax return in March 2022 and discovers that he has a liability of £1,000 for 2020/21, which he paid on 16 March 2022.

Because he paid his tax late, he is liable for:

- interest on the late paid tax

- a further 5% late payment penalty because the tax was still unpaid on 2 March (30 days late)

He could have avoided the interest charge and late payment penalty by paying his tax on time.

Had he agreed a Time-to-Pay agreement with HMRC by 1 April 2022, he would have avoided the late payment penalty, although he would still have had to pay interest on the tax paid late.

He will also face a penalty for filing his return late (see Tip 96).

98. Check Your Tax Code

Your tax code determines how much tax is deducted under PAYE. You should always check that your tax code is correct, as errors may result in too much or too little tax being deducted. Revised codes are sent out automatically after a tax return has been submitted and these essentially assume that taxpayer's circumstances remain the same. This may not be the case. For example, if you declare untaxed interest on your tax return, the auto-coding process will assume that you have this income in the following year and adjust the code accordingly. If this is not the case, you will find that you have more tax deducted under PAYE than you need to.

HMRC may also adjust the code to collect tax on savings income. This may be easier than paying it at the end of the tax year but is not for everyone. You do not need to have this collected through your code. Instead, you can ask HMRC to take the savings adjustment out of your code and pay the tax under the self-assessment system. This will increase your take-home pay each month.

Where an individual's income is over £100,000, the personal allowance is reduced by £1 for every £2 of income above £100,000. Where HMRC expect the allowance to be abated on the basis that the previous year's income was in excess of £100,000, they will take away the personal allowance from the tax code. If your income is likely to be less than £100,000 you can ask that they readjust the code, rather than waiting until you file your tax return to claim a repayment. This will provide a cash flow advantage.

If you do not think your code is right or it includes items that you would rather were dealt with via self-assessment, you need to contact HMRC. They should amend the code.

Problems may arise where a person has more than one employment. Check your code carefully.

Check Your Tax Code

Darren has a company car.

In April 2022, he changed his car to a more environmentally friendly model.

As replacement cars do not now need to be notified to HMRC on form P46 (Car) (although employers can provide HMRC with this information online if they want to), HMRC may not be aware of the change until his P11D for 2022/23 is submitted by 6 July 2023.

Darren's tax code for 2022/23 is based on his previous car and consequently, Darren pays more tax than he needs to each month as a result.

By checking his tax code and telling HMRC about the change, he will have more take-home pay each month.

99. Payments On Account

If your total net tax liability for the year is less than £1,000, or if at least 80% of the total tax due for the year is covered by tax deducted at source, then you do not need to make payments on account for the following tax year.

The second test is sometimes missed by HMRC and people are asked to make payments on account unnecessarily, resulting in a loss of the use of the money unnecessarily early.

Taxpayers can also elect to reduce their payments on account if they know that their liability for the current year will be less than the previous year.

Check your payments on account are not more than they should be. However, remember interest is charged if the payments on account are reduced to below the level that they should be.

Payments On Account

Robert calculates his tax liability at £7,000 for the year 2022/23, of which £1,200 relates to investment income payable under self-assessment. The remainder (£5,800) was deducted under PAYE.

Because his net tax liability is over the £1,000 limit, he assumes he has to make payments on account for the following year and hence enters these figures onto his tax return.

However, as over 80% of his total tax liability is deducted at source under PAYE, he meets the second test and does not need to make payments on account. The tax on his investment income is payable in full by 31 January following the end of the tax year. By being aware of this test, he avoids making payments on account and benefits from the associated cash flow advantage.

100. Watch Out For The Online Tax Calculation...

Where the tax return is submitted online, the associated tax calculation shows the tax due for the year, not the balance which needs to be paid.

Where payments on account have been made during the year, these need to be deducted from the liability for the year to show the balance due, if any, for the year of the return.

It is only this balance, plus the first payment on account for the following year, that needs to be paid by 31 January after the end of the tax year.

Chapter 13:
Final Tips

101. Register For Child Benefit

102. BONUS TIP Beware The Gift Aid Tax Trap

101.Register For Child Benefit

The high income child benefit charge applies where either a person in receipt of child benefit or his or her live-in partner (whether or not they are married or in a civil partnership) has income of £50,000 or more.

The charge is set at 1% of the child benefit awarded for each £100 by which income exceeds £50,000. Where income is £60,000 or more, the charge will equal the child benefit paid in the year.

Where the recipient of the benefit does not live with a partner and has income of £50,000 or more a year, it is the recipient who will pay the charge. However, where a couple live together, if only one person has income in excess of £50,000 that person will pay the charge. Where both parties have income in excess of £50,000, the person with the higher income will pay the charge. This means the person paying the income tax charge will not necessarily be the same person who receives the benefit.

It is possible for a couple each earning £49,999 (a total income of £99,998) to retain full child benefit, whereas a single person or a household with a single earner with an income of £60,000 will have to repay all the child benefit.

Where one partner has income of more than £50,000, redistributing income may enable the couple to retain their child benefit. Similarly, in a single parent household where income exceeds £50,000, reducing income to below £50,000 by, say, delaying payments from a family company, entering into a salary sacrifice or contributing to a pension, may allow child benefit to be retained in full. Keeping income below £60,000 if it is not possible to reduce income to below £50,000 will mean at least not all child benefit is clawed back.

Those affected by the child benefit tax can choose not to receive the benefit or can continue to receive it but pay it back in tax.

However, it is important to register for the benefit even if you elect not to have it paid, as National Insurance credits are given automatically to parents registered for child benefit for a child under 12. This will ensure that the year is a qualifying year for state pension purposes. A person needs 35 qualifying years for the full single-tier state pension and at least ten years for a reduced pension. This is something that should not be overlooked, particularly if one parent is a stay-at-home parent or on a low income and the other has income in excess of £60,000. Failing to register for child benefit can adversely affect state pension entitlement.

Register For Child Benefit

Henry and Paula both work in the family business. They have two children and receive child benefit of £1,885 for 2022/23 (£21.80 per week for the first child and £14.45 per week for the second child for 2022/23).

Henry has income of £65,000 and Paula has income of £25,000. The child benefit is paid to Paula. However, as Henry's income is above £60,000, he suffers an income tax charge equal to the full amount of the child benefit paid to Paula.

If they are able to reduce Henry's income to £45,000 and increase Paula's income to £45,000, the high income child benefit charge will not apply and they will be able to keep the full amount of their child benefit. This will give them additional income of £1,885 despite the fact that their combined income is unchanged. They will also save tax because more of their income will be taxed at the basic rate rather than at the higher rate (see Tip 6).

However, if they are unable to do this, Paula should remain registered for child benefit so that she benefits from the associated tax credit. However, they should elect for it not to be paid so that they do not have to pay it back in the form of the tax.

102.BONUS TIP: Beware The Gift Aid Tax Trap

Gift Aid allows charities to increase the value of donations made to them by enabling them to reclaim basic rate tax on the donation, as long as the donor signs a gift aid declaration confirming that he or she is a UK taxpayer. The donation is made net of basic rate tax. Where the donor is a higher or additional rate taxpayer, they are able to claim relief for the difference between the higher or additional rate, as appropriate, and the basic rate through their self-assessment tax return.

Many people make regular donations to charity and sign a gift aid declaration covering all gifts to the charity. This is fine as long as the donor remains a taxpayer, but it could cause problems if the donor's income falls or he or she ceases to pay tax as a result of an increase in the personal allowance.

The tax repaid to a charity on a gift aid donation is funded by the tax paid by the donor. If tax is reclaimed by a charity and the donor has not paid sufficient tax to cover the sum reclaimed, HMRC can recover the tax from the donor.

Those with low incomes should review gift aid declarations and cancel them if it appears that they will not pay sufficient tax to warrant the declaration.

Beware The Gift Aid Tax Trap

For many years, Pauline has given £10 a month to a particular charity. She has signed a gift aid declaration covering all future donations. Until 30 April 2022, she was employed on a salary of £30,000 a year. She retires on 1 May 2022. Her income for 2022/23 is £10,000, which is covered by her personal allowance. Consequently, she pays no tax in 2022/23.

Pauline will need to cancel her gift aid declaration and not gift aid any donations that she may make in 2022/23, to ensure that HMRC does not try and recover any tax reclaimed by the charity from her.

Lightning Source UK Ltd.
Milton Keynes UK
UKHW010006090622
404112UK00003B/98